London's Lost Pubs

LONDON'S LOST PUBS

SAM CULLEN

WHITE OWL
AN IMPRINT OF PEN & SWORD BOOKS LTD.
YORKSHIRE – PHILADELPHIA

First published in Great Britain in 2025 by
PEN AND SWORD WHITE OWL
An imprint of
Pen & Sword Books Ltd
Yorkshire – Philadelphia

Copyright © Sam Cullen, 2025

ISBN 978 1 39903 826 3

The right of Sam Cullen to be identified as Author of this work has been asserted by him in accordance with the Copyright, Designs and Patents Act 1988.

A CIP catalogue record for this book is available from the British Library.

All rights reserved. No part of this book may be reproduced or transmitted in any form or by any means, electronic or mechanical including photocopying, recording or by any information storage and retrieval system, without permission from the Publisher in writing.

Typeset in Times New Roman 10/12 by
SJmagic DESIGN SERVICES, India.
Printed and bound in India by Replika Press Pvt. Ltd.

Pen & Sword Books Ltd. incorporates the imprints of Pen & Sword Books: After the Battle, Archaeology, Atlas, Aviation, Battleground, Discovery, Family History, History, Maritime, Military, Politics, Select, Transport, True Crime, Fiction, Frontline Books, Leo Cooper, Praetorian Press, Seaforth Publishing, Wharncliffe and White Owl.

For a complete list of Pen & Sword titles please contact

PEN & SWORD BOOKS LIMITED
George House, Beevor Street, Off Pontefract Road, Hoyle Mill, Barnsley, South Yorkshire, England, S71 1HN.
E-mail: enquiries@pen-and-sword.co.uk
Website: www.pen-and-sword.co.uk

or

PEN AND SWORD BOOKS
1950 Lawrence Rd, Havertown, PA 19083, USA
E-mail: uspen-and-sword@casematepublishers.com
Website: www.penandswordbooks.com

CONTENTS

LONDON'S LOST PUBS

For hundreds of years pubs have played an intrinsic part in London life. Many excellent books have been written about them from a variety of different angles or themes but there is one aspect that has been neglected – the ones we've lost. That's not to say there hasn't been plenty of media attention about the plight of pubs, and regular newspaper and magazine articles have been dedicated to the trend of pub closures, both in London and further afield.

So that got me thinking: what about telling the stories behind these lost pubs, their history and the quirky tales about them and in turn their own contribution to London life as we know it? In short, that's what this book is all about.

Now anyone familiar with the latest stats about pub closures will know we've lost a huge amount across the capital in recent years (although not as bad as in some other parts of the country) and I've not been able to include every single pub that closed. If I'd done that you'd be looking at a book the size of a coffee table as opposed to a coffee table book.

My criteria for inclusion has been that they closed within the last twenty-five years (I've made a couple of exceptions for special cases) and there was an interesting story to tell. The latter point is inevitably subjective but to my eyes that includes historical events, features that were unique to a particular pub as well as architectural and design elements. I've included at least one pub from every London borough. I've also tried hard to give a good representation of post-war pubs which have been particularly hard hit by closures and in my eyes are more at risk of being forgotten than somewhere with the history of say Jack Straw's Castle.

I haven't included pubs which closed and have been replaced with another trading on the same premises but with a new look/identity. Had I done so, top of my list to include would have been the Sun and Doves in Camberwell, a buzzing pub run by Mark Dodds until a near doubling of the rent charged by the pub company owners ultimately culminated in him being evicted and declared bankrupt after he refused to pay the higher amount. Mark still campaigns vociferously to this day for a fairer deal for pubs. My other inclusion would have been Zeitgeist on Black Prince Road, a German pub full of German beer and German food in an old Victorian pub building. It was popular with Germans and non-Germans alike and a million miles away from one of those inauthentic theme places with bands and staff in Lederhosen. Both were favourite pubs of mine and neither has had their place truly filled on the London pub scene in my opinion.

In researching this book, I've consulted a wide range of sources, drawing on London pub guides dating right back to the early part of the twentieth century up until contemporary guides issued in the 1990s and 2000s. I've also drawn on online reviews of our closed pubs while they were trading and on occasion have been fortunate enough to speak to people involved with some of the pubs featured who've given me their recollections.

I appreciate that flicking through a book looking at pubs across the capital that are no more could potentially be viewed as a depressing read. However that's not how I see it. I've written this to celebrate the fact we had these pubs in the first place and to make sure they're remembered, in most cases with a smile, rather than lost to the mists of time.

In many instances I've also included details of valiant local campaigns to save beloved boozers; the good people at CAMRA and countless community associations deserve tremendous credit for putting in the hard yards to try and save so many pubs across the capital. In recent years this has been aided through the creation of the designation of 'Asset of Community Value' (ACV). While the pages here inevitably detail those in which the battle was lost, these organisations have equally saved so many others and I take my hat off to their perseverance in that regard.

It's not all one-way traffic, and there have been notable London pubs in recent years which have reopened after long periods of closure: spots like the Magdala and Olde White Bear in Hampstead as well as those which were converted into chain restaurants but then reverted back to pubs, including The Steam Packet by Kew Bridge.

It is also true there are a sizeable minority of the pubs featured here where the building remains intact and they could yet be revived. Indeed I love to think of someone reading these very words in a pub featured in these pages that has since reopened, and raising their glass to its revival!

The book is organised geographically for coherency and to make it easier to follow. In total there are 204 pubs featured, each with their own stories to tell. Where pubs have had multiple names over the course of their life, I have generally only used one in the header for their entry, with all their other names mentioned within the body of the text. On a small handful of occasions where I felt it was particularly necessary, I have included both in the header. I hope you enjoy this trip with me through the history of London's lost pubs. I certainly learnt a lot while researching it and I hope you do too while reading it.

Cheers!

Sam Cullen

ACKNOWLEDGEMENTS

In writing this book I have been fortunate to draw on the assistance, encouragement and wise words and pointers in the right direction from many good people. This list includes but is certainly not limited to:

Chris Amies, Edmund Bird, Jessica Boak and Ray Bailey, Cllr Tony Belton, The Cartoonist Club of Great Britain, Anne Gerrish at *Time Out*, Kim Godfrey, Gerry Hahlo, Peter Jacob, Jane Jephcote, Ewan Munro for his fantastic photo collection, Sofia Akram and Emma Anthony at the Wandsworth Archives, Roger Protz, David Ramzan, Georgina Wald at Fuller's, Rex Ward, James Watson and finally the multiple staff at the Westminster City Archives who retrieved old books for me on countless Saturdays!

In addition to those listed above there were many people who kindly spoke to me about their experiences at an individual pub featured in these pages and who are acknowledged in the relevant entry.

Thank you also to Time Out London for their agreement for me to use extracts from their *Time Out Pubs & Bars*/*Time Out Pubs, Clubs and Bars* Guides from 1998–2007.

PHOTO CREDITS

Many thanks to the below for agreeing that I could use their excellent photos in this book; the pages in which they appear are listed below. All the remaining photos were taken by yours truly!

Chris Amies – 25, 35, 118, 127, 159, 161, 163, 165

Des Blenkinsopp – 183

Matt Brown – 77, 122

Tim Brown – 5, 61, 154

Rich Cains – 128

Martyn Cornell – 107

Amir Dotan – 139

Malcolm Edwards – 33

Diamond Geezer – 179

Flying Saucer Draught Emporium, Texas – 103

Fuller's – 164, 167, 169, 172, 175

David Heath – 28

John Law – 166

Jim Linwood – 1

Lost Pubs Project – 113, 124

Vici MacDonald – 36

Ewan Munro – 6, 8, 13, 16-9,21, 23, 26, 29, 32, 41-4, 46, 48-50, 52,54, 59-60, 64-5, 67, 72,78,80-1, 83, 85, 86,90, 92-3, 95-100, 102, 105, 119, 125, 130, 132-3, 135-6, 140-5, 149-150, 156, 158, 162, 171, 176-8, 181, 186

Jessica Mulley – 112

Felix P Ormerod – 148

Matthew Rees – 109

Sarah Tan – 75, 84, 87, 89, 91, 137, 182

Rex Ward – 146, 170

CITY OF LONDON

THE CARTOONIST

76 Shoe Lane, EC4A 3JB

Located at the foot of Richard Seifert's imposing International Press Centre (IPC), The Cartoonist opened in 1973 and lived up to its name by serving as the meeting point of the Cartoon Club of Great Britain (CCGB).

It was the society's PR man at the time, Reg Orlandini, who heard that a pub was planned at the foot of the IPC and contacted the brewery St Georges to suggest calling it The Cartoonist. The cartoonists also contributed a unique feature of the pub – the sign changed every year and was designed by a member of the society.

While hosting the annual Cartoonist of the year award it played host to a wide array of political figures who'd been featured, including Ken Livingstone, Tony Benn (who referenced his visit in his diaries) and even Margaret Thatcher, albeit while she was still Leader of the Opposition.

It wasn't just the Iron Lady who dropped in here, they even hosted a grizzly bear in 1980! That year a bear called Hercules had broken loose up in Scotland while being filmed for an advert and the hunt to get him back became a major news story. As a result, the CCGB gave Hercules their 'Golden Joker' award for 1980 and invited him down for the ceremony. The City of London police weren't massively thrilled by this, especially when the bear was out of his cage, and told the club committee they'd all be arrested under the Dangerous Animals Act if Hercules wasn't back in his cage in thirty minutes!

The Cartoonist survived the great newspaper exodus from Fleet Street, having a brief spell as The Cartoon Page when it was part of the Front Page pub group. It kept flying the flag until early 2013 when it was rubbed out when the IPC was demolished to be replaced by the 1 New Street Square development.

DANDY ROLL

Gateway House, Bread Street, EC4M 9BR

The Dandy Roll dated from 1956 and was located on the ground floor of Gateway House, headquarters of the speciality paper manufacturer Wiggins Teape. This also inspired its name, a Dandy Roll being a piece of machinery used in the manufacture of paper.

In its early days this pub featured an extensive range of cheese for sale in its basement bar, including British staples such as Cheddar, Blue Stilton and Wensleydale, something which Alan Reeve-Jones thought couldn't help but make a visitor here smile.

It featured in the book *City of London Pubs* in 1973 where the authors Timothy M. Richards and James Steven Curl mentioned its nickname as the Randy Doll, something they speculated was a ploy to encourage Wiggins Teape employees to visit here. The Randy Doll nickname also ended up making it into this pub's entry in *The Wordsworth Dictionary of Pub Names* printed in the 1980s and 1990s.

The Wiggins Teape building was demolished in 1999, taking the Randy Dandy with it.

HORN TAVERN/CENTRE PAGE

29–33 Knightrider Street, EC4V 5BH

The earliest records of a Horn Tavern in this area date back to 1687. It had the honour of being referenced in Charles Dickens' *Pickwick Papers* as it was here that Mr Pickwick sent out for two bottles of good wine while he was incarcerated in the nearby Fleet Prison. For many years the pub displayed a bust of the great author in the bar.

The pub did well to survive both bomb damage during the blitz and the threat of demolition during redevelopment proposals for the area in 1967. What the pub failed to avoid was being renamed in 2002, to the Centre Page, as part of the Front Page pub chain. The Dickens/Horn connection was still referenced outside the pub which had Johnny Homer wondering why they'd bothered with the name change at all when he featured the pub in his 2016 book *City of London Pubs*.

The Front Page pub chain ended in the mid-noughties but curiously the new owners of the pub chose to keep the name rather than revert to the historic title. In this era you could also spot a signed photo of David Hasselhoff behind the bar, the pub playing on the Knight Rider street theme. The Hoff visited the pub in 2008 alongside Alan Carr.

I visited once in early 2022 and it felt a rather odd place, and any historical ambience which may have been there was obliterated by the bright lighting. The main group of customers were a group of overseas students who were all being served their dessert, some sort of custard dish, which further diminished the character and gave it more of a college canteen feel.

The Centre Page had closed by the end of that year which didn't really generate any publicity, which seems a bit surprising given its rich history. The building remains fully intact so a new chapter could yet be written here.

MAGOGS

8 Russia Row, EC2V 8BL

Built as a replacement for the earlier Gog and Magog pub on Cheapside that suffered bomb damage during the blitz, this was located underneath the Sun Life Insurance building.

The Magogs name was chosen to keep continuity with the previous pub, a suitable name for somewhere in the heart of the Square Mile, as Gog and Magog were the two legendary giants that were guardians of the City of London. Statues of these beasts can be found outside the Guildhall.

There were statues of both Gog and Magog outside the pub, as well as a clock inside where they both appeared ready to battle each other at quarter to the hour, like a City of London version of a cuckoo clock.

In its pomp there were three bars here, including a downstairs area with a DJ every lunchtime. In its final years it became part of the Vino Veritas chain which popped up in a number of former city pubs. It was then converted into a Pizza Express. The pub was demolished alongside the rest of the office complex in the early 2000s.

OLD KING LUD

12 Ludgate Circus, EC4M 7LQ

Dating from 1870, the Old King Lud occupied a commanding position on Ludgate Circus, located right beside the Ludgate Hill railway bridge. Regicide was almost committed one hundred years later when it was nearly demolished for a road expansion scheme at the Circus. These proposals were thankfully abandoned but in a pre-emptive move a replacement pub opened nearby called The New King Lud before the plans were dropped. The younger Lud was renamed as Bradys not too long after.

Like many pubs in the 1980s, the Lud had DJs in the evening to entice the punters. At one point this even included future TV entertainer and game show host Dale Winton. Recalling the experience in an interview with *The Sun* in 1996, Winton referred to it as 'the filthiest, dirtiest pub you've ever seen', adding that no DJ before him had survived more than two nights in the pub, but he lasted three months. The final straw for Dale was when he was clearing his stuff away one evening and accidentally disturbed someone who was sleeping in the corner of the pub and the man then came after him with a bottle.

At the start of the nineties, it was all change at Ludgate Circus as the railway bridge came down as part of the changes that saw the construction of City Thameslink and demolition of the old Holborn Viaduct station. The pub was shut for a period while building work took place around it with office blocks coming down too. The Lud reopened in 1993 and while looking the same from the outside, only the façade had been retained in the redevelopment and everything behind it was new.

By all accounts it was a raucous, rowdy place in this new incarnation, albeit one with an extensive beer selection. *Evening Standard* reviews of the 1990s referred to people frequently ordering four-pint pitchers of beer, as well as contests to see if anyone could drink thirty halves of ale in three hours! In 1999 the latest round of changes at the Lud even made the pages of the *Financial Times* where Peter Millar bemoaned the introduction of spurious metal ducting and bright continental lighting. Millar did however acknowledge these kind of wholesale changes were nothing new here as the pub had constantly been altered to whatever the 'image makers' thought the trend of the time was.

It then duly lost the final link to its old identity, its name, simply becoming one of many Hogshead venues in the Whitbread chain of the time. It didn't last long in its final guise as the pub closed in the early 2000s. The premises have been used as a Leon for many years now, although two figures of King Lud still remain above the entrance as a reminder of his reign here.

PRINTER'S DEVIL

98–99 Fetter Lane, EC4A 1EP

The Printer's Devil was one of several theme pubs which sprung up from the brewery Whitbread from the late 1950s onwards. Here the pub played tribute to the newspapers, the dominant trade of the time in the area, and walls were decorated with images detailing the history of printing as well as memorabilia from the trade. Whitbread even issued an accompanying book to catalogue all the items on the walls. The name derived from the nickname given to an apprentice in a printer's workshop but the inn sign had a bit of fun with the concept, showing a devil-like creature surrounded by letters from a printing press.

In 1962 Alan Reeve-Jones wrote that it was a 'showpiece' amongst pubs and that no visitor should omit it from their itinerary of a London visit, continuing to praise it by saying there were so few other pubs of such high order, marvelling at what in his eyes was effectively a permanent exhibition on 'the mystery of printing'.

Before its re-theming it had been known as the Vinters Arms with a history back to the 1820s. It sustained damage during the Second World War and the following renovation work ushered in the Devil's era.

The newspapers began to leave Fleet Street from the mid-eighties onwards but the Devil stood resolute on Fetter Lane until its print run ended in 2008. It was demolished five years later.

SHIP AND TURTLE

122 Leadenhall Street, EC3V 4QH

Through its multiple incarnations there were plenty of elements which made The Ship and Turtle unique amongst pubs in the City of London. Firstly in a period spanning over one hundred years it was run by a succession of five widows, one after another, from the mid-eighteenth century until well into the Victorian period. Then, when it was rebuilt during the latter part of the nineteenth century, it had water tanks with turtles swimming in them according to the book *Victorian Pubs* by Mark Girouard. It was then reconstructed again in the 1960s and was located at the bottom of the new P&O building. This time they had a fishpond in the main bar area which was thankfully covered over when discos took place here during the evenings!

In its later years it popped up in Nicholson guides where it was said to increasingly have the atmosphere of a wine bar, with no reference to the fishpond. In its final years it was renamed Vino Veritas, part of a small chain across the city. It closed in 2007 ahead of the demolition of the building, notable for the fact that the contractors started from the bottom up (while retaining the core of the building), so The Ship and Turtle would have been first to go.

THE SHIP TAVERN

27 Lime Street, EC3M 7HR

Two other vessels of the same name remain in the city; this one sailed off in the mid-noughties but is still very much worthy of a mention. This Grade II listed building dates from the mid-nineteenth century but records suggest there was a Ship pub in this location way back to the fifteenth century.

At the start of the 1990s the interior featured a ten-foot glass ship in a case, as well as a bar shaped like the side of a rowing boat, so they were certainly playing up their nautical theme. An online review in its final days in 2008 described it as a lovely traditional pub with wooden flooring and the seafaring theme well represented with stuffed fish and lanterns dotted around the place.

The pub closed a year later and you're now more likely to encounter chicken than fish as you'll find a Nando's here.

SIMPSON'S TAVERN

38 1/2 Cornhill, EC3V 9DR

This was a historic chop house which chalked up over 250 years of service just off Cheapside. It was first established in 1757 by Thomas Simpson, famous for running a successful fish restaurant in nearby Bell Alley, who was gifted the land for this tavern by his father.

In 1973 Curl and Richards called it one of the treasures of the city and an absolute must for the enthusiast. Its interior had wood panelling and communal tables. The upstairs was solely for enjoying the products of the chop house, with a downstairs bar and courtyard for those just seeking liquid sustenance.

It managed to reopen after covid and the slow return of people to the office. My one visit was on a Friday in August 2021. It was moderately busy and the staff I spoke to were hopeful that autumn would see more people coming back into the square mile and unable to resist the signature sausages which were recommended as a side for practically every dish!

By all accounts trade was returning to normal, when suddenly in October 2022 they were forced to close after being evicted by their landlords with no notice. As the managers of the pub said, they'd got plenty of Christmas bookings in.

This action triggered a significant backlash in the media. The City of London Corporation listed the building as an ACV. The managers of the pub then won a court battle against the landlord's attempts to wind up their company.

This victory wasn't enough to get the pub reopened as the landlords have still got the premises locked up. Maybe by the time this book comes out Simpsons will have reopened, and you can be sat in there, reading this and ready to enjoy their traditional culinary delights and the obligatory sausage.

STILL AND STAR

1 Little Somerset Street, E1 8AH

This pub first opened in 1820 and was considered the only slum pub in the City of London. A slum pub is where existing slum dwellings have been converted into a pub, in this case two slum houses combined together. It also has an impressive literary history, with Daniel Defoe reportedly writing sections of *Robinson Crusoe* here. It was also the only pub in the country to have the name Still and Star. This derived from the fact that when it first opened, they distilled spirits for the pub in the upstairs room. The star was a nod to the presence of a sizeable Jewish community in this part of London in the nineteenth century.

In 2016 it was revealed the pub was set to be demolished to enable the development of a large office block planned for the area. This triggered a vociferous campaign, strongly backed by both the Victorian Society and CAMRA, to save the pub. Initially these efforts seemed to bear fruit as the pub was listed as an ACV at the end of the year. The media coverage caught my eye and I visited during that summer. I really enjoyed the atmosphere here in this traditional, no-frills pub, with horse racing on the TV and a dart board on the wall, feeling a world away from the modern bars popping up under new developments in this rapidly changing part of the city.

The pub closed as a going concern in 2017 and despite its earlier designation, planning approval for its demolition was granted in 2020. These initial plans were altered, giving another chance for the pub to be saved, but this revised application was also given planning permission in April 2022. The artist's impressions show a replacement pub being constructed beside the imposing new development as part of these plans, but no doubt lacking the character the original building acquired over its 200-year lifespan.

TIGER TAVERN

Bowring Building, Tower Place, EC3P 3BE

Given it was located so close to the Tower of London, it only feels right that there are some impressive historical stories associated with this pub. Records of a Tiger Tavern in this area reportedly date way back to the start of the sixteenth century. It was rebuilt several times with its final version opening in 1965, located at the edge of a then new Bowring office block. They even got Field Marshal Earl Alexander of Tunis doing the honours for the official opening.

One of the earlier reconstructions in the late Victorian era had uncovered a mummified cat and collection of rats. There are two stories about the cat, both involving Queen Elizabeth I. One is the fact it was her pet when she had been incarcerated in the tower by her sister Queen Mary. Another similar story suggested the cat was actually the landlord's pet but that Elizabeth would come to visit it via a secret passageway that ran from the pub's cellars over to the tower itself. A niece of a manager of the pub during the 1980s has written online that she visited the tunnel during this period.

The pub also played host to an event once a decade where the Lord Mayor of London visited to check the quality of the beer. A slightly more left field part of the process was when the beer was then poured on a seat and another gentleman tasting the beer then sat on it. If their trousers then stuck to the seat, it was the sign of quality which would be marked by hanging a laurel garland over the pub sign.

The Tiger became extinct at the start of the 2000s with the demolition of the Bowring office block. The new resting place of the mummified cat is sadly unknown. Given it has been rebuilt several times before, I am surprised someone hasn't tried to resurrect it again.

WHITE HART

3 New Fetter Lane, EC4A 3BN

This was barely a minute's walk from the vast, imposing office block which was home to the *Daily Mirror* and *Sunday Mirror* from the late 1950s to 1994. As you might imagine, it became a haven for the staff working there and gained the nickname 'The Stab in the Back', due to the resentment certain Mirror staff had when their offices were moved here.

There are various riotous stories about the conduct of *Mirror* hacks while in 'The Stab', including the legendary author and columnist Keith Waterhouse threatening to put the landlady's pet chihuahua into a sandwich and even getting two pieces of bread ready.

The White Hart survived for a few years after the *Mirror* moved out, closing in 1999 as the building it was in was significantly remodelled. Its place was taken by Pizza Express which in turn closed shortly before the pandemic. The *Mirror* monolith was replaced by the glass curves of the Sainsbury's HQ so the area looks radically different from the era when the pub was in its prime.

The White Hart also has its place in history via its cameo in an archive news clip that can be viewed online. The short snippet features a press pack following Mark Lawrenson, who had just been sacked as Oxford United manager, exiting the *Mirror* offices after being given the news by club chairman and *Mirror* owner Robert Maxwell. Lawrenson heads over to the White Hart to drown his sorrows, only to find it hasn't opened yet. When he finds the door locked, he appears to check his watch, despite the fact he isn't wearing one.

THE WHITE SWAN/MUCKY DUCK

108 Fetter Lane, EC4A 1ES

This originally opened as The White Swan but was often known by its nickname of the 'Mucky Duck', and from 1993 it was renamed after its nickname for the best part of a decade.

In this persona The Duck included a choice array of traditional British saucy seaside postcards, living up to its Mucky name. Within a year of the renaming there were 264 of them decorating the walls, highlighting the particular talents of Donald McGill, amongst others.

By 2003 it had returned to the original name and was now a smart gastropub. When it appeared in the 2006 *Time Out* guide they noted features like the stuffed swan and ship's bell which helped bring 'old world solidity'. It also featured in a glowing article in the *Evening Standard* in 2010 where they noted the food offering which included a pint of prawns or even a pig's cheek.

The White Swan managed to make it through the choppy waters of covid only to close for good by 2021. There is a large new office block planned on the site of the pub which in theory includes the option for a replacement pub on the ground floor.

THE WHITE SWAN

28–30 Tudor Street, EC4Y 0DD

Another staple of the newspaper era on Fleet Street, The White Swan was the closest pub to the old *Daily Mail* building.

It was here in 1961 that the British lawyer Peter Benenson, alongside a number of his friends, founded Amnesty International, the international campaigning organisation for Human Rights. This fact was marked by a plaque on the pub's wall designed by Peter Jacob, a member of the CCGB and a regular presence at The Cartoonist mentioned earlier in this chapter.

In the 1970s Richards and Curl described it as being decorated with prints, cuttings and cartoons from newspapers so it was very much playing to the gallery of the local clientele. Interestingly they stated it was better known by the nickname of the Mucky Duck, much like another nearby White Swan on Fetter Lane. Here the pub even had a football team called the Mucky Duck XI.

The CAMRA review in 1991 noted the presence of authentic pub memorabilia here in the shape of a water pump which had been used to extract well water when the pub had been known as the White Swan Hotel.

The pub was gone by the end of the decade as part of a widespread redevelopment of the site of the former *Mail* HQ. The façade of the building has been retained and there is a small reminder of its past life in the shape of two stone white swans by the doorway.

WESTMINSTER

BALMORAL CASTLE

1 Churchill Gardens Road, SW1V 3AJ

This Victorian pub stood as a survivor from another era when the vast majority of the local area was cleared for the huge Churchill Gardens Estate. The retention of the pub was directly stipulated by the architects of the scheme, Philip Powell and Hidalgo Moya.

In 1969 Glyn Morgan referred to it as a 'homely and incongruous' village pub that acts as a 'natural focal point' in an 'impersonal living area'. It is certainly interesting how attitudes change as Churchill Gardens is now seen an exemplar piece of social housing and much of it has been Grade II listed. The Balmoral was praised in Mark Girouard's book *Victorian Pubs* for its set of ornate nineteenth century wall panels advertising amongst other things the 'Superior Old Irish and Scotch Whiskies' that were available.

The pub closed in the early 2000s but remained standing behind hoardings and scaffolding for the best part of 20 years. The wrecking ball finally came in 2022 as part of a Westminster City Council project to provide new supported accommodation and council housing.

THE BEEHIVE

7 Homer Street, W1H 4NU

This small cosy pub took its name from this area of Marylebone's former role as a major source of honey for London. You had to keep your wits about you as there was another identically named pub a short walk from here.

It appeared in Lynne Pearce's *London Pub Guide* from 2001 and on the author's visit to the pub she had the pleasure of seeing the late Wendy Richard holding court here, drinking 'Moët from a sherry schooner'. Pearce was very impressed by the

pub, noting the eclectic décor above the bar which included plastic pigeons and Chinese style vases and summed up by saying 'the beer is well kept, the banter is lively… the Beehive has true star quality'. Pearce also reckoned the pint-sized pub had barely more than thirty seats.

Apparently sightings of Wendy Richard were common here as a poster on the Lost Pubs website recounted she could be seen drinking champagne while sitting at the bar with her partner and a small dog!

The Beehive closed in 2014 and the site has remained derelict ever since.

CAPTAIN'S CABIN

4–7 Norris Street, SW11 4FU

Originally known as the Punch House, by the 1940s it had been renamed as The Captain's Cabin, which was also accompanied by the pub acquiring a nautical theme.

Appropriately enough it was a favoured haunt for the comedians recording the BBC naval comedy *Round The Horne* at the nearby Paris Theatre.

As the years went on it retained elements of its nautical theme. Reviews still online from various pub websites from the early noughties onwards are split between those who liked it as a slightly different offering from the rest of the Leicester Square pub scene and others who disagreed and thought it was a dull chain pub.

The Captain was ultimately usurped by the Crown as it was swept away in a comprehensive redevelopment of the Haymarket area by The Crown Estate, who owned the land, closing in 2013 and being demolished shortly after.

DANIEL GOOCH

40 Porchester Road, W2 6ES

This corner pub which opened in 1974 was located on the ground floor of the Colonnades, one of the first London buildings designed by the architects Nicholas Grimshaw and Terry Farrell, who went on to leave their mark on London's skyline with buildings like Waterloo International and the imposing office complex above Charing Cross station.

Talking of the railways, this pub was named after one of the engineers for the Great Western Railway during its early days under Brunel. This small, cosy pub had a loyal following amongst the local community. Its archive Facebook page displayed posts about pool tournaments as well as live football on big screens.

It closed in 2016 when the building was refurbished, and its ground floor position is now occupied by a lobby. Recent planning applications relating to the Colonnades still refer to the potential for a pub on the ground floor but it's hard to imagine now.

FEATHERS / SWAN & EDGAR

43 Linhope Street, NW1 6HE

Dating from 1899, this mini-Marylebone pub staked a claim to be the smallest in London. Peter Haydon and Chris Coe agreed with this assertion when they included it in their 2003 book on London's best pubs. Their view was that the pub couldn't even fit twenty people in.

In *Time Out*'s pub guide from 2000 they felt twelve people being in there was enough for 'a crammed, shoulder rubbing crowd' while mentioning the landlord's claim he got eighty people in to watch an England v Ireland rugby match. The reviewer went on to say they were 'silently glad' they hadn't been there to see it!

In its final incarnation it was reborn as the Swan & Edgar, the name of a former department store on Piccadilly Circus. It now sounded like it was going for the quirky gastropub vibe with the bar itself made up of books glued together with a plank of wood on top and the toilet walls decorated by Scrabble letters. Even the bill was delivered to the *Evening Standard's* reviewer within an old book.

The book closed on the Edgar in 2013. However, as multiple planning applications to convert it into residential use have been refused, there is still hope it could yet be taken off the shelf and opened once more.

HAND & RACQUET

48 Whitcombe Street, WC2H 7DS

Believe it or not, there was once a tennis court right by Leicester Square and it was that which gave its name to the pub here. It was first recorded in the seventeenth century and was rebuilt in the mid-Victorian era and it was in this incarnation that it enjoyed its heyday.

In the 1950s and '60s it was laughs being served up here as it became a haunt of many comedy giants of the time due to its location by the Paris Theatre, where leading lights such as Tony Hancock, Sid James and Tommy Cooper performed for BBC Radio shows and then visited the pub afterwards. It was viewed by many as a hidden gem, offering the chance for a peaceful pint away from the hordes of tourists at Leicester Square.

It closed in 2008 and spent several years derelict while various planning applications were submitted. Eventually one was approved and demolition began in 2015. While this was due to commence, an enterprising fan of the pub and the comedy stars that frequented it managed to save the eleven-foot sign that was once stuck on the front of the pub. He also found it a new home, the Museum of Comedy just near the British Museum, where it takes pride of place amongst other comedy memorabilia and trinkets.

HEROES OF ALMA

11 Alma Square, NW8 9QA

A pub that was popular with Britain's best-selling band of all time, the Heroes of Alma first opened in the mid-nineteenth century.

Its location very close to EMI's Abbey Road studios meant it was a natural refreshment point for the bands recording there, including most notably The Beatles. Sadly nobody has yet proved that the photo from the *Abbey Road* album cover was them on their way to this very pub.

The Heroes closed in 2002 and was converted into a house. *The Daily Telegraph* did a feature on it when the building was up for sale in 2011, interviewing the then owner Owen Taylor who said he'd once seen Sir Paul McCartney in a Chinese restaurant and asked him if he remembered visiting the pub. The man himself replied that he certainly did and the band had spent hours in there after recordings, with Taylor adding his own narrative that it sounded like the pub had been a 'central place' for the band.

It still attracts fans of The Beatles to this day, an easy follow up photo to get after snapping yourself using the crossing.

HOG IN THE POUND

28 South Molton Street, W1K 5RF

While the pub can trace its lineage back to the early eighteenth century, its final incarnation was housed in a modern, early 1960s building.

Its macabre claim to fame from its early days was that its landlady, Catherine Hayes, was the last person in Britain to be burned alive as a punishment for committing murder, after she poisoned her husband in 1726.

The pub relocated from its original site, thought to be the current location of Swallow Place, to the corner of South Moulton Street by 1806. This in turn was demolished by 1959 ahead of the final rebuild.

The distinctive name was thought to derive from the original use of the first building as a butcher's, which had its sign as a huge hog in a pound. The sign stayed when he departed and was kept for the pub, giving it its name.

The Hog's tale ended abruptly in 2011 when the building was demolished for a retail development.

THE INTREPID FOX

97–99 Wardour Street, W1F 0UF

This legendary Soho drinking den combined political cunning and rock star royalty during its long period of existence. First established in 1784 by Samuel House, the name originated from the fact House was a staunch supporter of the leader of the Whig party Charles James Fox and promised to give free beer to anyone offering to support him.

During the second half of the twentieth century, it was a favoured haunt of both rock bands and actors. The story goes that it was also the scene of a near confrontation between Mick Jagger and Rod Stewart, after the former was caught trying to tap up Ronnie Wood from Stewart's band The Faces to join The Rolling Stones. Other notable hellraisers who used to drop in included the actor Richard

Harris and The Sex Pistols. The pub's many fans were shocked when out of the blue at the start of September 2006 it was announced it had been sold to a property developer and was going to be replaced with flats.

The pub closed barely a week after the announcement so there wasn't much chance for the pub's high-profile supporters to mount a campaign to save it, despite securing the support of Malcolm McLaren, manager of The Sex Pistols at the height of their fame. In the end there was some small consolation as the building itself, complete with Intrepid Fox and Buxton beers tiling, was retained and converted into a chain of the Byron burger restaurant. Meanwhile The Intrepid Fox slunk off a little further west and set up shop several months later in a much more nondescript building underneath Centre Point. Unfortunately for fans of the Fox's second incarnation, lightning did indeed strike twice as this site was also acquired as part of a wider development of the St Giles area; this time the building was demolished and has been replaced by flats.

THE LORD HIGH ADMIRAL

43 Vauxhall Bridge Road, SW1V 2TA

It is not uncommon for pubs to be Grade II or even II* listed, as you'll see from many examples in this book; however what is much rarer are post-war pubs that have received that accolade.

The Lord High Admiral falls into that category. It first opened in 1969 on the ground floor of one of the blocks of the Lillington Gardens estate, an excellent piece of architecture from a social housing perspective and a nice reminder that not all blocks were concrete in this era. It was designed by John Darbourne, the architect for the entire estate. It inherited its name from the Victorian pub it replaced.

It made regular appearances in the Nicholson pub guide throughout the 1980s and '90s where its popularity with tourists and the quality of the lunches were referenced in the reviews. The pub itself was listed in 1998, with English Heritage calling its design of 'exposed brick' and 'timber boarding' characteristic of the period and serving as an 'exceptional example' when it was first built, and a remarkable survivor from this era.

In later years it was known by the rather generic name of 'Pimlico Beer Garden' and latterly it was a branch of the 'Moo Cantina', an Argentinian steak restaurant. I walked past it on several occasions in this guise and now wish I'd popped in, if only for a Quilmes, to admire the interior. For some reason I never particularly felt like a steak at this end of Vauxhall Bridge Road so I was never drawn in.

Moo had closed by 2023 and here's hoping it reopens as some sort of pub or restaurant in the future so I can atone for previously missing it!

LOWNDES ARMS

37 Chesham Street, SW1X 8NQ

This pub dated from 1829 and was built by Paul Dangerfield who was also responsible for the Duke of Wellington pub nearby.

Alan Reeve-Jones provided a suitably colourful review from the 1960s when he described it as a place where 'Gentlemen instinctively remove their hats on entering', as well as remarking on the bar's 'soft pink lights and frilly boudoir curtains'. Reeve-Jones then pulled back from suggesting it was a den of iniquity by saying that the pub was most respectable with customers of high regard.

It appeared in the British film *The Crying Game* in 1992 where two of the protagonists met to discuss a planned assassination in a movie which was called a 'brilliant IRA thriller' by the BFI. In 1994 it was praised in *The Independent* for having one of the best pub gardens in London, described as 'real city garden sunk deep in a well of high houses'.

In the late 1990s the pub was under threat which triggered a high-profile campaign to save it, including stars like Sir Alec Guinness. Ultimately though this failed to generate any new hope for the pub and it had closed by the end of 1998, being converted into housing in 2003.

THE PAVIOURS ARMS

Neville House, Page Street, SW1P 4BG

Based on the ground floor of Neville House, an office building which opened in 1937, the Paviours featured an Art Deco interior in keeping with the style of the time. What wasn't in keeping was the fact that this interior survived intact throughout its existence with the fixtures and fittings all retained.

Its unique aesthetic saw it as a regular fixture in London pub guides, with *Time Out* in 2002 reserving special praise for the dining room with its 'silver and black lacquered dining tables', 'deco lamp standards' and a 'curved glass lighting feature' which they said was enough to take your breath away.

At the start of the 2000s, Neville House was up for demolition. This triggered a vociferous campaign to save the pub. A BBC News article at the time referred to it as 'London's most complete Art Deco pub'. Given its proximity to Parliament, a group of MPs even put down a Parliamentary motion calling for its preservation. Sixty-seven MPs put their name to the motion, including future Labour leader Jeremy Corbyn, although if at that point someone had said he'll be Labour leader in twelve years' time, they'd probably think you'd had a few too many ESBs at this Fuller's managed pub.

When I spoke to Colin Challen, the former MP who tabled the motion, he said it was getting a bit run down towards the end but that he felt the interior should definitely have been preserved, even if it involved moving it. He said it was a spot he liked to go to chat to other fellow 'old' Labour MPs who could voice their displeasure at Tony Blair in the Art Deco surroundings.

Regrettably the campaign was unsuccessful, and Neville House and The Paviours was demolished later that year.

PIG AND WHISTLE/GROUSE AND CLARET

15 Little Chester Street, SW1X 7AP

This was built in the 1960s as a replacement for a pub on the site called the Stanhope Arms which was damaged during the blitz.

It featured in Martin Green and Tony White's 1973 *Guide to London Pubs*, where they noted that it was a popular spot for Sunday lunchtimes, when it was at its 'gayest', a theme that Green returned to in his own solo 1982 pub guide where he noted it was a gay pub 'on the international scene'. It was renamed in 1987 as The Grouse and Claret. In its entry in various *Evening Standard* guides the authors speculated the change had been triggered by a feeling that the earlier name didn't seem in keeping with this well-heeled part of Belgravia.

By the early 2000s it was run by the brewery Hall and Woodhouse, with a Swedish restaurant on the first floor, giving a curious Dorset/Scandinavian fusion.

It had closed by the start of 2008 and was converted into flats.

PONTEFRACT CASTLE

73 Wigmore Street, W1U 1QB

This mid-nineteenth century pub spanned over four levels with a cellar bar and two floors dedicated to dining above the main pub area.

This was another pub Alan Reeve-Jones visited in the 1960s and was particularly impressed with the pub's dining room, stating Louis VIX would approve of the fare on offer. It then popped up in a guide to London pubs sponsored by Alka-Seltzer no less. This referenced the popularity of the ground floor bar where punters spilled out onto the streets during sunny weather.

At the start of the nineties, it was praised in the Nicholson pub guide as an 'exuberant free house' with flowery painting outside, while for the interior they mentioned antiques, sea-chests and of all things, Victorian porn. This was not referenced in their later guide in 1995!

The pub shut down in 2015 and the building was demolished, with the façade of the pub retained at the front of the new building.

PRINCE OF WALES/SWAG AND TAILS

10 Fairholt Street, SW7 1EG

This Knightsbridge mews pub began life as The Prince of Wales in 1831 and in the post-war period boasted a bevy of famous customers, including Boris Karloff.

In the early 1980s it was reportedly managed by Sid James' brother and in the last year of that decade renamed the Swag and Tails, referring to the type of curtain in use at the pub. However it equally sounds like something Sid himself might have said as a bit of cockney innuendo.

It became a suitably classy gastropub in keeping with the neighbourhood and was summed up in the 2004 *Time Out* guide as a 'free spirited pub', which 'serves its well brought up clientele perfectly.' In its appearance in the previous edition of the book, the reviewer had mentioned trying hard not to be distracted by the presence of Bernie Ecclestone here. It's ironic they mentioned the Formula 1 mogul as six years later his daughter Tamara acquired the pub.

Ecclestone had bold plans for the Swag but quickly irked neighbours by her plans to demolish and rebuild the pub to triple its capacity and keep it open later at weekends and assuming that getting planning permission was a formality. Westminster City Council refused and the row then took a surreal turn. The Ecclestones began talking of converting it into a fish and chip shop, even putting a neon fish and chips sign in the window of the derelict pub to further irritate the neighbours.

The Ecclestone plans ultimately went nowhere but the Swag and Tails was not revived, being demolished in 2013 and replaced by flats.

THE RED LION

1 Waverton Street, W1J 5QN

Dating back to 1749, this Mayfair mews pub first opened for the servants that worked for the wealthy residents of this district, in line with how public houses were viewed in that period. As time moved on, the pub became a haunt of the well-to-do locals as well as people working in the area.

It was a regular feature of pub books during the 1960s and '70s with some suitably evocative descriptions deployed, a favourite of mine being Alan Reeve-Jones' description of the dinner here as 'soft with languid comfort'. He also reflected that the quiet forecourt of the pub during summer 'encourages al fresco ruminating after a superb lunch'. High praise indeed!

This view was still evident in the early noughties where Haydon and Coe remarked the pub 'exudes a certain casual gentility', with its one-man settees, wood panelled bar and artefacts dotted around the place. It regularly appeared in *Time Out* guides, although in 2000 they noted fish and chips cost £14.50, an eye-watering amount back then and for many years after too!

The Monopoly board doesn't lie, Mayfair is one of the most expensive parts of town so the pub was a prime target for property developers. It closed in 2009 and the relatively intimate pub was transformed into a huge townhouse, with only the façade of the building retained. This sold for an eye-watering £19 million in 2014. The owner then had it repossessed and it was sold on for £15 million in 2018, described as a knock down price in the *Daily Mail*. I suppose everything is relative.

ROSSETTI

23 Queens Grove, NW8 6HJ

A true one-off, Rossetti was an Italian themed pub. It arrived in the 1970s, replacing the Rose and Crown, a Victorian era pub.

Photos of the outside suggest a fairly unremarkable post-war low rise building but it was the inside where the Italian spirit ran wild, with marble counters, tiled floors and statues of Roman and Greek heroes. The name came from Dante Gabriel Rossetti, a nineteenth century poet and painter who had lived locally.

Summing up his view of the pub at the end of the eighties, the legendary Roger Protz waxed lyrical about it as somewhere 'blazing with passion and joie de vivre', a place to savour and enjoy.

After the longstanding landlords left in the early 1990s the pub didn't last much longer and was demolished. It was replaced by new faux Victorian housing which at least references the pub in its name of Rossetti House.

THE STAG

15 Bressenden Place, SW1E 5DD

As London roads go, Victoria Street seems in a state of constant flux. Buildings constantly coming up and down, many with a relatively short shelf life.

The Stag falls into that bracket. Built in 1962 as part of a redevelopment of the site of The Stag brewery (incredible to think of a brewery on Victoria Street!), this octagonal flat roof pub popped up alongside a set of office blocks adjacent to Victoria Station.

In the early 1990s it was noted as having a games room upstairs, and by the end of the decade it became a gay pub with cabaret nights, DJs and drag acts.

It was still going strong in this respect when in 2011 it was confirmed it would be demolished as part of yet another Victoria Street redevelopment project. The curtain came down in March 2012, not before there had been a series of buzzing farewell events which were then brought together on a DVD sold by the management.

THE TAVISTOCK ARMS

41 Tavistock Crescent, W11 1AD

This first opened in 1873 under the name the Tavistock Arms and ended up closing with that name in 2009, although there were plenty of changes in between as well as an appearance in a classic cult movie.

At the start of the 1980s, it became the Frog and Firkin, the third venue in David Bruce's Firkin pub chain which were known for brewing their beer on site and which subsequently swelled in size over the course of the decade.

It earned its place in cult immortality when it featured in the 1987 film *Withnail and I*, where it was called the Mother Black Cap, no doubt inspired by the Black Cap pub in Camden.

It churned through different names at a rapid rate from the late 1990s onwards including Frudruckers, Barbushka and a spell as the Mother Black Cap. It had reverted to its original name by the time it closed in 2009.

It was demolished for flats in 2012. On learning its fate, the *Withnail* director despaired and asked why the 'ghastly' Trellick Tower hadn't been demolished instead. As a fan of Goldfinger's hulking great tower, I'm afraid I must disagree with Bruce Robinson there.

TOWER TAVERN

21 Clipstone Street, W1W 6BA

Opened in 1970 and named after the BT Tower which it stands in the shadow of, the pub by contrast was in a flat roof, low rise building. It replaced a pub which was called the Fitzroy Arms, dating back to 1826.

This felt a slightly bizarre pub on my first visit in 2007, where there was a brightly lit interior with high bar stools and blinds which felt more in keeping with a 1970s office development. It was late in the evening so I might not have seen it in its best light. I only visited once more, in 2016, when it had a bit more atmosphere and was busy with students from the nearby Westminster University.

The pub's website in 2018 talked about the Tower's 'glistening white tile exterior' with the look in keeping with the brutalist style of the time, although the text was never ultimately filled in when it was designed, with the date left as XXX!

It never reopened post-covid. The building remains fully intact, shuttered up with the glistening white tiles discolouring with the passage of time, leaving the door ajar for the tower to rise again.

WINDSOR CASTLE

27–29 Crawford Place, W1H 4LJ

This began life in the mid-nineteenth century as the Gloucester Brewery and Beer House, being rechristened to its longstanding name a few years later.

It entered its magisterial phase in the 1990s under the reign of Michael Tierney. Reopened by Wendy Richard (clearly tempted away from The Beehive) at the start of the decade, this ushered in an era where the pub was renowned for its unique interior. Appropriately given its name, it was chock full with royal memorabilia with the walls covered in prints of the family as well as a host of other trinkets like ashtrays! When

Peter Haydon reviewed it in 2009 he described it as a 'superbly English pub' where you'd be 'spirited away to a land of deference and good manners'.

On the first Friday of the month, it was also a land of impressive 'taches as it served as the meeting point of the Handlebar Club with their impressive array of facial hair.

It closed in 2016 but much of what made the inside so memorable has been transferred lock, stock and barrel ten minutes west to The Heron pub on the Hyde Park Estate. This included not only royal mementos but the Handlebar Club too. The pub sign for the Windsor Castle has been preserved and can be found in The Heron's small back garden.

KENSINGTON AND CHELSEA

ADMIRAL BLAKE/THE COWSHED

355 Ladbroke Grove, W10 5AA

This originally opened as The Admiral Blake and while it was known as this for much of its life, there was a spell when it was called The Cowshed and it was in this guise it gained national exposure.

The pub was used as the exterior location for *Time Gentleman Please*, the Sky One comedy starring Al Murray as Guv, the pub landlord. It was never referred to by name in the show, instead always being referenced as the 'Pub by the chemical works'. The one exception being an episode where the guv wants to rename the pub as the Cow's Head as a slight against his enemy from the brewery, Vicky Jackson. However he spells it incorrectly as The Cow Shed.

Despite its brush with national stardom, the pub closed in 2009. It was demolished in 2012 and replaced by a block of flats called Admiral Blake House, property developers clearly thinking Cowshed House wouldn't project the right image.

THE AUSTRALIAN

26 Milner Street, SW3 2QF

This lost pub took its name from the presence of the former cricket ground, Princes, which was located just to the north of the pub. It was at this ground that a touring Australian team first took on England at cricket in 1878, twenty-three years before they were even an independent country, hence the name.

While the ground didn't last much longer after the match and was built on for housing four years later, the Australian pub enjoyed an extended stay at the crease. It was a regular staple in London pub guides throughout its life, featuring in most guides issued from the 1960s onwards. The *Evening Standard* review from 1998 is typical of them, praising the pub as being like a 'perfect museum of cricket' given all the memorabilia that had been accumulated here and an 'extraordinarily pretty pub' on account of the creeper growing outside and its various hanging baskets.

The Australian's innings came to an end in 2006 and it was converted into an interior design shop.

THE BLENHEIM

27 Cale Street, SW3 3QP

Positioned halfway between Brompton and King's Road, the pub first opened in 1824. In the 1980s Martin Green described it as a 'warm, two bar pub', with the reviewer particularly happy with the wood panelling, something he saw as a relief in an era of plastic.

The pub was damaged in the 1987 hurricane when a chimney went through the skylight of the back bar. It then closed in 1991 for two years before being

taken on by a local businessman who got in church lanterns from Halifax, oak floorboards from a French railway carriage and even old radiators from County Hall to decorate the place. This didn't succeed and it closed before being taken on by Hall and Woodhouse, with new landlords Tony and Lynn O'Neill giving the place a cheerful, buoyant air, with all this information recounted in the 1999 *Evening Standard* guide.

This cheerful, buoyant air didn't last long as the pub closed in the early 2000s. It survived plans to convert it into a single house (which would have been quite the pad given it's a four-storey building). It became a high-end restaurant in 2006 called Tom's Kitchen, the Tom being Michelin-starred chef Tom Aitkens. This lasted until 2021 and now the premises are up for rent.

THE ENNISMORE ARMS

2 Ennismore Mews, SW7 1AN

A small mews pub, its first incarnation dated back to 1845 but was destroyed during the Second World War. It was rebuilt and reopened in 1958.

By the 1980s it had acquired a reputation for fine food and even received praise from the leading gourmet of the time, Egon Ronay. It was also known as a haunt for certain stars of stage and screen, most notably Charles Grey, Blofield in *Diamonds are Forever* and The Criminologist in the *Rocky Horror Picture Show.*

The curtain came down on The Ennismore in 2002 and, despite CAMRA's best efforts to save it, the pub was demolished and replaced by flats.

KENILWORTH CASTLE

104 St Annes Road, W11 4BU

This is without question one of a kind. The original Kenilworth Castle pub was demolished after the Second World War and a replacement opened as part of the construction of a nearby housing estate, Henry Dickens Court. And what a replacement, with an exterior looking more like a Charles Holden tube station than any standard pre- or indeed post-war pub.

In an image from 2012 which the photographer kindly allowed me to reproduce here, the modern exterior seems in contrast to the traditional green signage which looks like it could have been off the Rovers Return. Fred Elliot meets Walter Gropius.

It closed as a pub two years later but thankfully we're still all getting the dividend of this excellent piece of architecture as it was saved, albeit converted into a Co-op, so at least this one-off piece of pub design wasn't lost.

KING'S HEAD & EIGHT BELLS

50 Cheyne Walk, SW3 5LR

This pub can claim an impressive lineage back to the fifteenth century, although the present Grade II listed building dates from the early nineteenth century. The double-barrelled name, appropriate for these parts, comes from the fact it began life as two separate pubs serving those working on the river. The King's Head was for the officers and the Eight Bells for the crew.

By the Victorian era it was a favoured haunt of the many painters residing in Chelsea, living on Cheyne Walk and nearby streets. This included the American artist Whistler, whose paintings of the river by Battersea Bridge can still be viewed at Tate Britain.

During the 1940s it was also one of Dylan Thomas's favourite haunts, a man who certainly liked a pub or two. In the swinging sixties it was a favourite of a different type of poet, Mick Jagger, who was now living on the prestigious street.

It held out as the last pub standing on Cheyne Walk until early in the new millennium when it was closed and converted into a French restaurant. It is now a high-end British eatery called No. Fifty Cheyne.

MAN IN THE MOON

392 King's Road, SW3 5LR

A Chelsea institution which was arguably best known for its impressive theatre. By the turn of the 1990s the Nicholson guide labelled it London's most comfortable pub theatre on account of the quality of its upholstered seating.

By all accounts the interior overall was very impressive with large cut glass mirrors and decorative tiling. The pub saw its fair share of characters over the years, reportedly being a haunt of Christine Keeler, the woman at the centre of the Profumo scandal. Another account online on the Lost Pubs website from Helen Dodds states she saw Phil Lynott from Thin Lizzy there propping up the bar one lunchtime in the early 1980s. It also had its fair share of local eccentrics too, including a chap called Fred who managed to make it into the pub's entry in the *Evening Standard* guide published in 1994. Fred was a loyal customer here for fifty years and regularly sank ten pints a day. In the edition published two years later, they remarked the upheaval in the pub had caused Fred to take his custom elsewhere.

The pub had refurbishments in the late nineties costing around £250,000 which were hoped would turn the Moon's fortunes around. These hopes turned out to be ill founded as the Moon closed in 2002, never to return. It reopened in 2003 as a restaurant called Eight Over Eight, which is a Chinese proverb meaning lucky forever. Fans of the pub's interior would have felt a definite irony in that name as the original features, including the theatre, were entirely gutted in the process. The restaurant wasn't lucky forever either as it didn't last long before being replaced as various different entities had a go at taking on the site. At the time of writing it is unoccupied.

THE MOORE ARMS

61–63 Cadogan Street, SW3 2QP

A proper Knightsbridge corner pub which first opened in the 1840s.

Former landlady Wendy Reakes kindly spoke to me about her time here and explained it was a key haunt on the Chelsea/Sloane Ranger scene of the 1980s. Regulars included a young Tara Palmer-Tomkinson and the pub was even mentioned in a *Tatler* article. By the mid-1990s it seemed to have a slightly different vibe as it was referred to by Peter

Haydon as a good honest working class local. He went on to explain that while it was frequented by businessmen during the day, it became a haunt for those from nearby social housing in the evenings and at the weekends there wasn't 'a Rupert or Fiona in sight'.

By the turn of the millennium, *Time Out* felt the pub was bland and lacking character. It didn't last much longer and was closed and converted into flats in 2003.

THE QUEEN'S ELM

241 Fulham Road, SW3 6HY

You may be starting to detect a theme here but this was another Chelsea pub popular with the artistic community. A pub with this name here is said to date back to 1667 and the current building is of a 1914 vintage.

It really came into its own during the extended period landlord Sean Tracey spent at the helm. David Hockney was a regular visitor and later the likes of Bob Geldof. Tracey even wrote a book about his time running the pub, *A Smell of Broken Glass*. The Alka-Seltzer guide to London pubs from 1976 pointed out not only the impact of Tracey's character on the pub but also interior features such as one of the largest collection of antique pipes in the UK, which had been amassed by Tracey, as well as cartoons by the celebrated satirist Jax.

The times were a changing when Tracey passed away in the late 1980s. His closing remarks at the end of his book included a hope that the pub would not end up as a mock 'Orish' pub like those that had started to pop up by the 1970s. I think the reality may have depressed him even more, as midway through the 1990s it had been reborn as Mwah Mwah. It's not only the name that would have raised eyebrows as the decor included tribal swords and shields. The *Evening Standard* pub guide for 1997 remarked that the staff still called it the Queen's Elm when answering the phone, given it would feel a bit silly to answer the phone and say 'Mwah Mwah Hello?'

It was goodbye to Mwah Mwah by the early 2000s as the building was converted into shops.

SIX BELLS

197 King's Road, SW3 5EQ

With origins in the early eighteenth century, the remaining mock-Tudor frontage Grade II listed building dates to 1898. During the first half of the twentieth century it was known as the 'Six Bells and Bowling Green' on account of that leisurely sport which was playable in the pub's sizeable garden. By the 1950s and '60s it played host to 'Trog's Jazz Club', featuring the up-and-coming names of British jazz.

In the 1970s the pub found itself subjected to a 'theme' experiment, when the main area of the pub was converted into the 'Birds Nest'. For the uninitiated, this

was an idea to try and open pubs up to get more female customers and then in turn, male customers, keen to pick themselves a nice girl from the Kings Road, as Des O'Connor once recommended in his old 'favourite' Dick A Dum. If you wanted to avoid all that fun, the pub did still have a large back garden, minus the bowls.

The Birds Nest experiment ended in 1983 and the following year it became Henry J. Beans, an American Bar and Grill with an interior the *Evening Standard* referred to as 'An American vision of a London Pub'. In due course Beans popped up in other locations across London, the UK and eventually further afield.

This had longer staying power than the Birds Nest but it too eventually succumbed, closing in 2013. The building is now an out and out restaurant as part of The Ivy chain.

THE SHUCKBURGH ARMS

47 Denyer Street, SW3 2LX

This Chelsea pub hit the headlines when the owners Scottish and Newcastle decided to rebrand it as part of their Irish pub chain Finnegan's Wake (back in the days when O'Neills wasn't considered more than enough…).

Wake seemed an appropriate epitaph for this ill-fated move as locals stayed away from the pub in protest and the move even provoked the wrath of the Shuckburgh family the pub was named after, especially when, according to the *Evening Standard*, the replica of their family crest attached to the side of the pub was thrown in a skip.

The original name was soon reinstated and the brewery invited along the Shuckburghs to mark the occasion and show off the reinstated family crest. Sir Rupert and Lady Shuckburgh politely told *The Standard* that while they liked the pub, the wrong crest of arms had been used.

The pub had been in the news earlier on in its life. Nina Challenor, daughter of the landlords Rob and Sadie Macdonald who ran the pub in the seventies, told me about how in 1975 the *Sunday People* did a feature on the pub's dog, called Sooty, who'd started to help walk slightly tipsy regulars back to their houses when it was closing time.

It closed in the early 2010s and the Grade II listed building now houses a delicatessen.

TEA CLIPPER

19 Montpelier Street, SW7 1HF

Beginning life as The Talbot in 1841, this backstreet Knightsbridge boozer was rechristened as the Tea Clipper in 1975 and duly filled with pictures of that type of boat. It was regarded as a safe haven for anyone wanting to escape the retail hedonism of nearby Harrods.

The pub popped up in an *Evening Standard* article in 2003 after some financial journalists heard the then landlady gloating about the struggles of nearby pub rivals such as the Bunch of Grapes and the Audley. I'm not sure how that ever passed for news but her indiscretion clearly irked those journos.

In the late noughties, the pub's website made the uplifting claim that the pub offered 'the warmth and pride of Britain in its most quintessential form' as well as a 'joyful vibe given off by both the locals and staff' which they were sure would keep people visiting again and again. The photos from this period show that the nautical pictures had survived well into the twenty-first century.

The tide went out on the Clipper in 2014 and the Grade II listed building was converted into housing.

THE TRAFALGAR

200 King's Road, SW3 5XP

This was originally called The Lord Nelson before being renamed after his most famous battle in 1971. By the 1990s it sounded like a buzzing hotspot. Featuring big screen TVs, pinball tables and other arcade machines alongside more traditional pub pursuits like darts and pool, the then manager proudly stated 'We would not be out of place on Blackpool promenade', according to the *Evening Standard* guide published in 1996.

I visited in 2018 and I'd certainly say the Golden Mile vibes were not evident, with it feeling like a typical London gastropub. They did, mind you, provide the best customer service I've ever experienced from a London Pub. On my first trip, I'd gone here to get some dinner, having checked the menu online and thought it was the most reasonably priced of the local options. On arrival I discovered this was out of date and prices had risen considerably, something more noticeable back then. It was a bitterly cold day around the time of the 'The beast from the east' so I ended up staying anyway. I emailed the pub afterwards to raise the issue of the old menu prices. The manager promptly replied to apologise and offered me a two-course meal for two with drinks on the house.

I naturally took him up on it and then duly told people how much I thought of The Trafalgar as a result. It shut later that year, which I stress was due to demolition of the building rather than the impact of my endorsement.

THE TOURNAMENT

344–346 Old Brompton Road, SW5 9JU

Dating from the mid-1960s and named after the Royal Tournament held every year at the Earls Court exhibition centre opposite, this replaced an earlier pub called The Richmond Arms which stood here.

It was one of the handful of London pubs featured on commemorative cards issued by owner's Whitbread. This one stated it had become a favoured meeting point for people from Australia, New Zealand and South Africa which they thought could be to do with Stella lager being available on draught. By the 1980s it was reported to be sporting a military themed interior.

The pub closed in 2011 and was demolished five years later, the initial planning application lapsing due to inactivity. In its last days it was squatted by Spanish anarchists, of all people.

SOUTHWARK

THE BEEHIVE

60 Carter Street, SE17 3EW

The Beehive is a remarkable survivor as it was the only building left standing on Carter Street after the Second World War. The present building dates from 1827, replacing another which had stood here from the mid-eighteenth century. A V1 flying bomb hit the street on 23 June 1944 and while not all the buildings on the road were destroyed by the initial blast, those that remained were so damaged they were subsequently demolished.

It featured in a handful of the *Time Out* guides at the turn of the millennium. One referred to the presence on the wall of a copy of the '*Daily Mail* front page telling of Thatcher's downfall', something they speculated was there to 'inspire the workers… at Labour's HQ'. During the 1980s and '90s the party had offices on the nearby Walworth Road so it would have definitely been a convenient watering hole for staffers.

In pre-emptive action to safeguard the pub, it was listed as an ACV in 2015 which was then renewed in 2020. The pub closed at the start of the first covid lockdown and has not reopened since. An attempt by the pub's owners to convert it into flats was refused by Southwark Council in November 2021 and the battle to save the pub goes on.

THE BLUE EYED MAID

173 Borough High Street, SE1 1HR

While the present building dates from the mid-nineteenth century, it is said there has been a pub called The Blue Eyed Maid located here since the late 1600s. Borough High Street has a rich history of coaching inns from the era when it served as the main route out of London to Kent and The Blue Eyed Maid has its place in that history. It was mentioned by Charles Dickens in *Little Dorrit*, putting it in the same company as other historic inns such as The George and The White Hart. It was so synonymous with the coaching trade that a vehicle actually ended up being named after the pub, with The Blue Eyed Maid coach offering journeys from London to Dover during the Victorian period.

During recent history, The Blue Eyed Maid was known for having one of the latest closing times of any of the pubs along Borough High Street. It also offered karaoke so you had to balance whether you fancied one more for the road against the variable quality of those stepping up to sing their hearts out in the early hours of the morning. It was trading right up until the first covid lockdown in March 2020.

The doors have remained firmly closed ever since but it remains fully intact with signage, so there could still be another song left in the old girl yet.

THE CHARLIE CHAPLIN

26 New Kent Road, SE1 6TJ

Named after arguably the local area's most famous son, the pub opened in 1965 at the same time as the adjacent Elephant and Castle shopping centre. The man himself even dropped by for a brief visit in 1972 which was captured as part of an Associated Press video detailing Chaplin's visit to London.

In 1983 it seemed as if the entertainment bug tendencies had rubbed off on the pub's landlord. The *South London Press* reported that the sixteen stone Mick Evers challenged Catweazle to a wrestling match to raise £500 for Guy's Hospital. Sadly the results of the bout were not carried in the following issue's sport section.

CAMRA gave the pub a mixed reception in a review in the eighties, praising the food and bare floorboards on one hand then providing a stinging criticism to the pub's aluminium and formica doors which they said was more akin to 'entering a post office'. The pub managed to avoid being painted in a garish pink colour in the nineties, a fate which befell the shopping centre.

It featured in the 2008 book *The Rough Pub Guide*; this wasn't meant as an insult in the style of the *Crap Towns* book, as the authors Paul Moody and Robin Turner were paying homage to a set of quirky, old-school pubs full of character. Although in this instance I think the pub's entry might be close to tipping into the other category, as the authors referred to the regulars as 'a motley collection of drunks, dipsos and the generally merry' who 'engage in the sort of apples 'n' pears banter Guy Ritchie dreams of'. This is followed up with a reference to an overheard conversation where a man says he's just back from prison in Thailand, having done four years inside which was originally meant to be fifteen but he 'got a royal pardon'.

The esteemed chroniclers of twentieth century pubs, Jessica Boak and Ray Bailey, visited in late 2017 and looked back at the history of the Chaplin in a blog post. From examining the promotional material issued by the brewery Watneys when the place first opened in 1965, their view was the original plan was that the pub would be serving the clientele of the shopping centre, which was initially hoped to be a high-end affair full of optimism and promise. When the centre ended up failing in its original lofty aims, the Chaplin ended up serving as the estate pub for the huge Heygate development which opened in 1971.

The show for the Chaplin ended in January 2018 when it closed ahead of the demolition of the Shopping Centre, itself part of a huge redevelopment of the wider area that had begun in the late noughties. When the closure date was announced, the final manager Craig Morrison wondered where his regulars would go as he didn't feel there were any other local pubs left in the area.

THE CROWN

115 Brandon Street, SE17 1AL

A traditional boozer tucked away just off the Walworth Road, The Crown served up pints here for over 120 years.

In 1996 Peter Haydon summed up the pub nicely by calling it 'something of an oasis' in an area not particularly well served with good pubs and that it offered a 'genuinely warm welcome'.

It came under threat in 2010 when developers were eyeing up the site for a block of flats. A 'Save the Crown' campaign quickly got going with the local community rallying around and support also coming from the then London Assembly Val Shawcross and local ward councillor Darren Merrill.

CAMRA's Jane Jephcote was quoted in the *Southwark News* article stating that 'We do not know of a better example of Brewery Tiling in London' and looking back

at photos you can certainly see her point. The dark coloured tiles are reminiscent of the oxblood colour seen across so many Leslie Green tube stations in London.

The developers got their way and the pub closed the following year and was demolished in 2014.

THE DUN COW

279 Old Kent Road, SE1 5LU

Formerly one of many pubs on the Old Kent Road, there are now only two left trading. The Dun Cow began life in 1856 as a multi-roomed gin bar. The present building here dates from a 1930s rebuild.

By the 1970s and '80s it had established itself as a venue both for live music and comedy, with acts very much of the era such as Bernard Manning, Mike Reid and even Jim Davidson before he got his big break. Martin Green painted a colourful picture of the place in 1982, with reference to pink furnishing, plants and even 'narcissistic mirrors' in the downstairs bar, while the upstairs was decked out in an Art Deco style.

Like many pubs on the Old Kent Road which also doubled up as nightclubs/live music venues, the Dun Cow was able to open till 2am at weekends, a rarity these days but nigh-on unheard of in the era where 10.30 or 11pm was the standard for all pubs across the country. This helped contribute to the place getting a reputation for trouble. A 1988 article in the *South London Press* referring to a neighbouring

pub's woes mentioned that the Cow had been able to hold onto its licence through introducing a lifetime membership fee for the princely sum of £20, enough to keep the authorities at bay.

In later years it was more of a champagne bar before being put out to pasture for good in 2004. The building was retained and converted into a GP surgery.

THE FROG AND NIGHTGOWN

148 Old Kent Road, SE1 5TY

Originally known as The Brunswick Tavern, this nineteenth century pub was rebuilt at the end of the 1960s and renamed The Frog and Nightgown. The off the wall name came from a fictional pub in the radio comedy *Ray's A Laugh* from the previous decade.

When Martin Green and Tony White wrote about the pub in 1973, they suggested the place was looking forward, not back, being light and airy with live music six days a week, implying it was more the kind of place to show off a Benidorm suntan rather than share hop-picking stories from days of old.

The landlord in the early 1990s, Ronald Hartigan, found himself in a spot of bother after finding an ancient atlas in a plastic bag by the bar in 1993, a document which had been stolen from a museum in Ireland two years previously. He then kept hold of the atlas for another sixteen months before coming forward. The thirteenth century artifact was subsequently returned to the museum and Hartigan charged with 'theft by finding' and sentenced to 120 hours of community service.

In the nineties it found a new lease of life as a pivotal venue for the burgeoning UK garage music scene, aided by its proximity to the massive club Ministry of Sound. The pub would open at 9am in time to catch the revellers as they poured out of the club. Live DJ set lists from the pub during this period can be found on YouTube as well as Spotify playlists for UK garage music which are named after the pub.

Its final metamorphosis was into the nightclub Virgo, which had closed by the late noughties and was demolished in 2014, with flats built on the site.

THE GROVE

520 Lordship Lane, SE22 8LF

Once referred to as occupying 'a major entrance to Dulwich', The Grove has a long history but decidedly uncertain future. The first pub with this name here opened in the 1860s with the present building dating from the 1920s.

In 1972 it was a finalist for pub of the year under the landlady Mrs Faulkner who decreed everything should be the best and served up a lavish carvery which led one local newspaper report to say they'd never seen so much turkey! In the following decade the pub had a small selection of animals based in the garden such as rabbits and guinea pigs to keep children entertained. This included a pet sheep who had been given the cheeky name of mint sauce and apparently liked Hoffmeister lager.

By the mid-1990s it was trading as part of the Harvester brand of pub carvery restaurants. In 2014 there was a major fire in the kitchen which led to it closing and the building has been in a semi-derelict state ever since.

Various plans have been brought forward for the site, including a care home. The present owners of the lease of the pub, Stonegate, contract with the Dulwich Estate doesn't expire until 2025, which one person speculated is giving the Estate time to formulate their long-term plan for the site. For their part Southwark Council have made it clear they would like a pub to remain here. At present the main hive of activity here is via a skatepark which had been built in the old car park by local skateboarders during the tail end of the first covid lockdown.

KING'S ARMS

132 Peckham Rye, SE16 4LJ

The original pub here opened in 1878 but was destroyed by a bomb during the Second World War, which tragically also resulted in the death of eleven people who'd been sheltering in the cellar during the air raid.

The rebuilt pub opened in 1957 with a distinctly 'Festival of Britain' architectural style. By the 1980s various stories were swirling around that the place was haunted by the ghosts of those who died when the bomb hit the pub. It featured in the 1987 book *The Haunted Pub Guide* which detailed the story of a former barman who claimed to have heard an 'old time sing-song' with a piano playing coming from the cellar.

It was latterly known as Kings on the Rye before closing in 1999. The building was retained but heavily modified when converted into flats. Its distinctive brick frontage was concealed by a white finish and the large windows reduced in size, taking away its period charm.

LONDON & BRIGHTON

141 Queen's Road, SE15 2ND

I will admit author's prerogative here, as someone who has only ever lived in London and Brighton, there was no way I was going to miss this pub out.

Not a huge amount has been written on it over the years, its only reference within Ron Woollacott's 2002 book on *Nunhead and Peckham Pubs* is that at least

the original owners went for a slightly more imaginative name than yet another Railway Tavern. The explanation here being the company which first built the line running through Queens Road Peckham was called the London, Brighton and South Coast Railway.

I popped onto the Peckham Remembered Facebook group to see if anyone had any memories of the place. The consensus view was that it was very much an old school pub. One poster remembered playing in a punk band there which had been slightly out of keeping with the usual vibe.

The pub closed down in 2008 and was squatted for a spell where the occupants put on gigs in the derelict building before being demolished in 2013. The sign however has been retained, so a portrait of Brighton's Royal Pavilion still looks out over Queen's Road.

PRINCE OF ORANGE

118 Lower Road, SE16 2UH

Dating back to 1859, the good Prince really got into his stride in the 1970s and '80s when it became known as a popular jazz venue. The biggest name to play here was Jools Holland in his early days as well as other jazz musicians such as Andy Graham and Chris Barber.

The late 1980s CAMRA guide entry said the pub came highly recommended, with a very high turnover of real ale as well as the jazz delights. They also noted the beer being pricey but thought this was understandable given there was no entry fee to see the big-name jazz on offer.

At the start of the following decade it got what can only be described as a rapturous write up from David Gammell who called the pub 'a jazz freak's dream' with an atmosphere as close as you could get to a 'New Orleans Honkey Tonk'. Gammell's creative juices were flowing for this entry as he was also transfixed by the audience in attendance for the live music, remarking how they 'weave, shake and snap fingers… in time to the beat'.

In its later years it had a brief change of style into a gay venue before closing at the tail end of the 1990s. It's been converted into flats which are known as Prince of Orange Court but the pub style frontage and two signs proclaiming the original name have been retained on its exterior.

THOMAS A'BECKET

320 Old Kent Road, SE1 5UE

The most famous of Old Kent Road's former pubs, the present building dates from 1898 but it has been suggested an inn with this name has been on the site since the fourteenth century. In the 1960s the first floor was used as a boxing gym by the legendary Henry Cooper, and Mohammed Ali heads up an impressive roster of boxers, including Joe Frazier and Sugar Ray Leonard, who also dropped in during its peak period. Under the helm of former boxing promoter Gary Davidson, the pub acquired the air of a boxing museum/hall of fame, with memorabilia such as a pair of Ali's gloves from the time Cooper knocked him out.

When it featured in the first two editions of the *Evening Standard* pub guide during the mid-1990s, The Becket was down on its luck and the author Angus McGill referred to it as effectively being in a permanent state of crisis, with a regular cycle of the pub looking on the brink of extinction only for a saviour to appear at the last minute before the pattern repeated itself. By 1995 he said things had got so bad the pub was only opening on Friday and Saturday nights for live

music. The following year he felt more enthused by the latest new management here who had got the place open every day again.

It didn't appear in the final two editions of the guide and spent a good proportion of the noughties closed. It reopened in 2011 which is when I saw it and to my eyes the then owners had done a decent job of freshening the place up while maintaining its heritage. Sadly it wasn't long before it closed again. Fears for the building's future saw it listed as an ACV in 2015 before the premises reopened in 2017 as the Rock Island Bar and Grill, complete with Frank Bruno at the opening ceremony. This too didn't last long before being counted out and was replaced in 2019 as a Vietnamese restaurant called Viet Quan. This survived the tumultuous covid period and is still trading today.

THE TWO EAGLES

27 Austral Street, SE11 4SJ

An imposing and impressive Victorian pub building, this structure is guarded by four decorative stone eagles found on its roof.

People reminiscing about the pub online from the sixties onwards fondly remembered it as a welcoming and friendly local, where there were regular piano players with everyone encouraged to join in the fun. Although the pub was just over the border into Southwark, Peter Walker still included it in his North Lambeth guide from 1989 and was very complimentary, praising its interior and features like cut glass doors and wood panelling, elements which Walker felt would justify the pub being awarded listed building status.

The pub closed in the late 1990s and has subsequently been converted into apartments, with the building renamed Two Eagles House. In autumn 2023, one of these dwellings was listed online on the Domus Stay website, an organisation offering luxury holiday lets. The apartment is marketed as 'distinguished yet playful' (aren't we all?), set within 'a local icon'.

WIBBLEY WOBBLEY

Rope Street, SE16 7SZ

This floating pub had a previous life as a ferry on the Rhine before being converted into a pub in 2001 by the alternative comedian Malcolm Hardee.

Given his background, it was no surprise open mic comedy nights were a staple here. Four years into running the pub Hardee tragically died after falling off a dinghy after a night in the pub on the way back to his own houseboat nearby. The pub continued under the reigns of his son Frank, brother Alex and Chris Luby, a fellow comedian. It appeared in the 2005 *Time Out* guide where the reviewer called it 'surprisingly low key and tranquil', with retro tack and nautical knick-knacks as well as a Wurlitzer jukebox packed with blues, jazz and ska.

I made a visit out here in March 2008. I remember it having a laid back, homely vibe but was feeling a little drunk after only one pint because of the boat's gentle rocking. I also recall a charming pub cat on the deck.

The Wibbley Wobbley closed in 2014 and had a spell occupied by an anarchist group before it was towed away from Surrey Quays to be scrapped. It is still held high in Londoners' affections and was referenced in a 2022 *Londonist* article about London's most missed pubs.

LAMBETH

THE CHEEKY CHAPPIE

89 Vassall Road, SW9 9NH

Opened in the early 1970s, the Cheeky Chappie was named after the early twentieth century music hall star Max Miller. It was a popular pub in the local Kennington and Oval areas before being demolished at the end of the 1990s, a very brief run in the pub world.

For some time after the pub was demolished, the sign remained outside what was now a health centre and flats. Eventually the signpost was felled and the sign itself ended up in a skip, destined for the tip.

Luckily someone spotted this and got in touch with the Max Miller Appreciation Society based in Brighton. One of the group raced into action, making the journey up the A23 to salvage it from the scrapheap. It's now more of a cheeky chippy as it can be found on the wall of Bardsley's fish and chip shop in the seaside city, as part of their permanent Max Miller exhibition.

THE CRICKETERS

17 Kennington Oval, SE11 5SG

Although this was a stone's throw away from The Oval, this place is more famous for its spell as a live music venue during the 1980s. In this period under the promotion of Jim Driver, a wide array of bands played here from The Pogues to T'Pau and even the first ever London gig of the Happy Mondays in front of a mere thirty people.

The music ceased in 1990 because of wholesale changes triggered in the pub industry through the Thatcher government's Beer Orders, which were intended to break up the monopoly of the breweries and saw the major companies having to sell off a vast amount of pubs. This saw the creation of new 'pub companies' (often shortened to PubCos) who were not connected to any brewery. In the case of The Cricketers, it was sold to the newly established Inntrepeneur.

The pub then changed hands and management multiple times with little success until closing in 2002, ironically just before the England cricket team reversed years in the doldrums and began an upturn in form that saw them finally win an Ashes series in 2005 after an eighteen year wait.

Attempts to demolish the pub in 2007/8 were refused by Lambeth Council but with wholesale redevelopment of the area around The Oval on the cards, approval was granted in March 2019 for its replacement with housing and a new replacement pub on the ground floor.

THE GEORGE AND DRAGON

16 Vauxhall Street, SE11 5LU

On first glance, The George and Dragon looked like a fairly typical London pub, built in a brick style similar to the interwar housing blocks off that side of Black Prince Road. However, for a brief spell it had a very unique claim to fame – it had a swimming pool in the back garden!

The pool was installed in 1983 after the pub was taken over by Julie Lettern, who ran it with her husband Brian. Unsurprisingly this generated a fair bit of media attention and was even featured on the local ITV Thames News, in an item which can still be viewed on YouTube. Julie is interviewed in this piece and explains that some of the pub regulars helped build the pool for them.

One of the locals is then interviewed, explaining it is mainly used by kids but that it's open to adults from 7.30pm to 9pm which is when they can 'all have a right laugh'. When the interviewer quizzes him about what they get up to when the kids aren't in the pool, he assures him 'no hanky panky' in a very London accent!

The Thames piece ends by saying next on Julie's list is a gym, sauna and jacuzzi. None of these transpired and when the pub was mentioned in a 1989 guide to pubs in the area, it references the 'ill-fated swimming pool'. The CAMRA guide to south east London pubs of the year before called it called it a 'very popular and boisterous two bar pub', again with no reference to a swimming pool.

The pub itself closed in 2006 and for several years afterwards the sign that boasted 'The only pub with a pool!' was still visible. The building has since been converted into flats, with no evidence as to whether they decided to put a swimming pool back in.

THE HERO OF SWITZERLAND

142 Loughborough Road, SW9 7LL

This curiously named pub (after William Tell, who was depicted on the inn sign) opened in 1962 within the shadow of the Loughborough Estate which had been built a few years earlier.

It was a rare survivor of the style used in new build local pubs at the start of the sixties. CAMRA's heritage listing for the pub drew attention to the difference between the public bar and the lounge area, with the former having a plain timber front to its bar and the latter having a plusher, padded panel version. The mosaic flooring around the side of the bar was also highlighted as a particular delight.

The Hero caught my eye on my first visit to this area in 2007, mainly due to its unique name. I finally got round to going in several years later and it was a perfectly amiable locals pub. I remember a sign up saying that if you were here to watch sports and not drinking, there would be a £10 charge, suggesting changing drinking habits in the area. It wasn't a sports night when I dropped in so I didn't see the policy in action, although the pool table was very popular mind you.

In 2019 Lambeth Council approved plans for demolition of the pub for a new thirteen-storey housing block, with developers promising a replacement pub on the ground floor. The Hero never reopened after closing for the December 2020 covid lockdown. Over two years later the building remained intact, if derelict, with the original pub sign removed (the developers referenced retaining the sign so one hopes it is safely in storage somewhere) and the site slowly filling with weeds and graffiti. While it will be something if the new building does include a replacement pub, it is highly unlikely to have the unique appeal and interior features of the Hero. CAMRA have called for as much of the historic internal features to be preserved but this isn't something the council were able to enforce.

LORD MORRISON OF LAMBETH

142 Loughborough Road, SW9 7LL

Pubs are very rarely named after living people, let alone living politicians, but the brewery Whitbread thought Herbert Morrison, former leader of the London County Council and a Cabinet Minister under Clement Attlee, was a sound bet.

They even got the man himself along for the official opening in October 1962, alongside a horse-drawn dray from the brewery. The story behind it being named after Lord Morrison was that he previously worked for Whitbread and was held in 'such affection' and 'pride' by them that they decided to name a pub after him. The pub's arrival was covered in a cartoon in the *Daily Mirror* newspaper by the artist Stanley Arthur Franklin, which had the pub filled with Tories throwing darts at a board with Morrison's face on it.

In later years the Lord Morrison suffered a greater ignominy as it became a strip bar called Red Stiletto and later Stockers, a tapas bar, and finally a brief stint as Flash Bar (strippers again) before closing in 2013 and being demolished for flats shortly after.

KING OF SARDINIA

21 Somers Road, SW2 2AE

Able to trace its lineage back to the 1870s, the present building has reigned since 1935.

It picked up the nickname as the King of Sardines amongst the locals. It closed in 2003 and was featured in a retrospective piece in the summer of 2020 from the local news website called *Brixton Buzz*. The piece included memories from former visitors to the pub, from those with benign memories like seeing a Brazilian jazz band playing on their first visit here to less favourable experiences like the presence of a miserable barmaid who seemed to have a thing against other women coming into the pub. CAMRA's mid '90s visit to the pub caught it in the middle of a refurbishment, where both a traditional and modern (i.e. arcade machines) games room was referred to.

The building has since been converted into housing and featured in the book *Lambeth Architecture 1914–1939*, with the authors describing it as 'a riot of well detailed decorative features', drawing particular attention to the 'barley sugar chimney', in two very evocative descriptions of the place.

THE LAMBETH WALK

17 Lambeth Road, SE1 7DG

At its peak there were several pubs dotted along this famous street immortalised in the song from the musical *Me and My Girl*. They've all closed now; this was the last one standing which is why I've picked it above the rest.

As The Masons Arms, the pub had roots back to the early nineteenth century, with the present building dating from around 1890. It was damaged in the Second World War and when its renovations were finished in 1951, it also sported a new name, now sharing it with the street it served as the gateway to. This change was accompanied by murals inside the pub depicting cockneys doing the 'walk' which made the street famous. In 1982 Martin Green reflected it had a 'strange period flavour' to it. Later in the decade Peter Walker wrote in *The Pubs of North Lambeth* that it had lively staff and clientele, as well as noting the amusing photos on the walls of staff and customers on days out.

Shortly before it closed it featured in a 2010 blog post on Lambeth pubs, the author remarking that it had a moribund air due to broken windows on the upper floors. It closed not long after and was converted to housing the following year. The Lambeth Walk signage has been retained, albeit with the exterior features of the building painted in a more neutral grey than the dark green scheme it had at the time of closure.

OLD FATHER THAMES

12 Albert Embankment, SE1 7SP

Located on the ground floor of Queensborough House which opened in 1956, this replaced the Red Cow which had stood here since 1815.

Old Father Thames featured in a handful of London pub books during the 1960s and '70s, with reviewers praising the interior with its murals of the Thames riverside in the sixteenth and seventeenth centuries, contrasted with photographs of the same view in the 1960s. There was also a wine bar located in the basement of the building, called the Old Tug.

This stretch of Albert Embankment had previously been full of office blocks but as the noughties progressed these began to be demolished and replaced by hotels or luxury housing blocks. Old Father Thames and Queensborough House, which was built as headquarters for the National Coal Board, was one of the first to go, being cleared in 2002 and replaced by the Park Plaza Hotel.

THE PILLBOX

199 Westminster Bridge Road, SE1 7UT

This opened alongside the Island Block, the 1960s extension to the GLC located on the traffic island by Westminster Bridge.

Like the block, the pub was a hexagon shape and they sought to continue this theme in the interior too, with hexagon shaped tables. The office block itself had a short shelf life as it became vacant on the abolition of the GLC in 1986. The pub, however kept going for a good twenty years longer.

Its original name could be seen as a tongue in cheek reference to the concrete construction of the building being like the pillboxes erected across the British coast during the Second World War. It had a spell as the Geoffrey Chaucer before finally being renamed as The Florence Nightingale in reference to the proximity of St Thomas's Hospital. Peter Walker's view from 1989 was that it was efficient and quite busy but not very pleasant. He also went on to complain about the tiny size of the gents' toilets so that may have cast his mind against the place.

In its final days the pub found itself heaving on a momentous occasion. It was Saturday 15 February 2003 and the march against the potential Iraq War. With most other venues nearer to the main rallying point of Hyde Park closed, the management here realised they could be well placed to serve the thirsty protestors. They called in all the staff they could, including Helen Thompson, then married to the landlord, who'd never worked behind a bar in her life.

It closed two years later and was swallowed up in the wider redevelopment of its long derelict neighbour into the Park Plaza Westminster Bridge.

WANDSWORTH

THE BEAUFOY ARMS

18 Lavender Hill, SW11 5RW

This traditional mid-Victorian era Battersea boozer gained a new lease of life during the 1980s when it became home to a thriving lively reggae music scene. One of the men on the decks in this era was David 'Ram Jam' Rodigan, a reggae DJ on Capital Radio. It also had a menu of Caribbean food including jerk chicken and curried goat. The fun didn't stop there either as they also had 'exotic dancers', at least that's the euphemism used in certain pub review books of this period.

In 1998 they had a bid for a later licence to stay open till 2am throughout the week turned down. A young Wandsworth Councillor called Sadiq Khan (whatever happened to him?) was quoted in the *Wandsworth Guardian* saying that 'the application caused a great deal of concern among local residents'. Talking of concern, in 2007 the pub was in the news again as an armed gang entered, mugged someone but were then repelled by the regulars pelting them with chairs.

In later years it was known as the Beaufoy Bar but the Caribbean theme remained. It closed in 2012 and the ground floor has been converted into a yoga studio.

THE CASTLE

115 Battersea High Street, SW11 3HS

There have been two pubs of this name on this site on Battersea High Street. The first reportedly dated all the way back to 1600, although it is unlikely much of this building remained by the time it was demolished to allow for the construction of council flats. Shortly before the demolition of the old building in 1963, there had been lots of interest in its wooden pub sign, which had only recently been rediscovered in 1950. The then landlord told local newspapers that he'd been offered thousands for it by American tourists.

That sum would have made for a nice nest egg for anyone, which is strangely ironic as workmen then discovered a hoard of gold coins as they were in the process of demolishing the old pub. After going through the proper processes, these were classed as 'treasure trove' and made their way to the British Museum. Two coins were retained by Young's (the brewery who owned The Castle) and were buried underneath the foundations of the new pub.

The new pub opened in 1965 with the much-coveted old wooden sign also taking pride of place outside. The foundation stone also included the estimate of a price of a pint in 1600 and then in 1965. The Castle's second incarnation proved popular and it often featured in London pub books right up until the 2000s. A recurring theme was how writers praised the character of the pub and contrasted that to the 1960s architecture which was frequently belittled. A particularly creative example of this came from *Time Out*'s review in 2002 which stated that while the pub was 'uninspiring outside, inside it is as warm and welcoming as a St Bernard in the snow'. Peter Haydon was also a fan of the pub through various editions of his guides but also disliked the building, calling it a 'first class example of unspeakably bad 1960s architecture'.

My only visit to the pub came in the summer of 2010, where I witnessed an unspeakably good goal by Giovanni Van Bronckhorst in the World Cup Semi Finals. Sadly, the second iteration of The Castle was not long of this world and was itself demolished in 2013 and the pub replaced by a modern block of flats. As the pub had been listed as an ACV shortly before it closed, this should have in theory seen the provision of a third version of The Castle on the ground floor of the new block. These plans were never realised and today the space is used by a children's nursery.

THE CASTLE

270 Putney Bridge Road, SW15 2PD

Another former Castle pub in Wandsworth and again, another which was part of the Young's family. Like its Battersea counterpart, the Putney incarnation can trace its lineage back hundreds of years. On this occasion, the first references to a pub of this name here go all the way back to 1758. It was taken on by Young's in 1831 and was expanded in the 1880s.

In 1935 the first Castle was demolished, to be replaced by a new build which opened three years later. This building lasted barely three years before it was hit by a bomb during the blitz on 19 April 1941, resulting in the tragic death of fifty-three people. The pub then traded again via a temporary building for many years until finally a new Castle was opened in 1959.

This third and final Castle reigned until closing on 3 March 2003. The pub was acquired by St George and demolished as part of the Putney Riverside development. A new Young's pub was provided as part of the development but this time they opted for a fresh start with The Boathouse which opened a year later.

THE CHOPPER/BATTERSEA BAR

58 York Road, SW11 3QD

Opened during the 1970s and for some time adorned with a model of a plane on its flat roof, this pub was located a stone's throw away from Battersea Heliport, London's only facility for helicopters.

In its twilight days it was rechristened as the Battersea Bar and into the new era it was featured in a glowing piece in the *Wandsworth Guardian* in 2010 stating the new managers had given the place 'a new lease of life' as a 'vibrant live music destination' known for 'top quality food'. The piece also featured a supportive quote from the owners, Admiral Taverns, stating that they were sure 'the business will continue to be a thriving success'.

This didn't last much longer sadly as the building was acquired by a property company in 2013. It was then derelict for a few years, changing hands between property companies before the new owners demolished it in 2019. It has been replaced by a fourteen-storey block of flats.

THE CRANE

14 Armoury Way, SW18 1EZ

This staked its claim to be the oldest pub in Wandsworth as it dated back to 1748, although the building itself was partially rebuilt in the 1920s. Given its proximity to the former Ram brewery, it's no surprise it was a Young's pub. It was also claimed to be haunted by not one but two ghostly figures, a small boy in knickerbockers haunting the bar and a lady in the attic who passes through the walls.

It largely went below the radar of the plethora of archive pub guides I consulted with the one exception being Roger Protz who praised the pub in 1989 for feeling like a country inn despite its location near the constantly busy South Circular Road and called it a 'delightfully unspoilt street corner boozer'.

It was rechristened as The Armoury for a spell in the 2000s, before returning to its original name when it was taken on by the Ram Pub Company, Young's offshoot company for its tenanted pubs. I visited here on a handful of occasions in the late 2010s and found it to be a friendly, welcoming pub despite its slightly unpromising location by the main road.

The pub survived the immediate aftermath of covid but closed down at the end of 2021, following on from Young's announcing they was largely winding down the Ram Pub Company.

HABERDASHERS ARMS

47 Culvert Road, SW11 5AU

Dating back to at least 1871, the Haberdashers survived the comprehensive redevelopment that took place across this patch of Battersea in the 1950s and '60s.

In the late 1980s, its side wall was enlivened by a bold mural by the celebrated local Battersea artist Brian Barnes. Brian got permission from the owners of the pub, Taylor Walker, to put a giant mural on the wall, called Battersea in Perspective. The result was the eye-catching views of Battersea, featuring an aerial view of the local area that centres in on Battersea Park and its peace padoga, alongside a collection of Battersea's former radical MPs from John Burns through to Alf Dubs at the bottom of the mural. It was officially opened in August 1988 by Lord Douglas Jay, himself a former MP for Battersea North for nearly 40 years.

In 2001 the then landlady, Maureen Courtney, told a local newspaper it was a 'no frills community pub where everyone knows everyone' as part of a feature on the pub. She was back in the paper later that year with a call for assistance in getting in touch with Brian Barnes to see about the prospects of getting the mural cleaned up. The word got back to Barnes who returned to the pub to give his work a bit of a spruce up.

The Haberdashers closed in the early 2010s but Barnes' mural remains in pride of place on the side wall.

THE HIGHWAYMAN

13 Petersfield Rise, SW15 4AE

This former pub dated from 1959, built shortly after the imposing and latterly Grade II listed Alton East estate on Roehampton Hill with the intention of serving the residents of these new flats. It featured in the 2008 CAMRA book *London Heritage Pubs – An Inside Story* by Geoff Brandwood and Jane Jephcote, who stated it had 'simple, angular architecture, typical of its day'.

The authors had a sense of tough times ahead for the pub when they remarked how one of its two rooms was now disused, an indication of changing habits in the area that had led to several pub closures already. The Highwayman succumbed to this fate a year later. The building survived until 2014 when it was demolished and replaced by flats.

Its name harked back to the history of the local area, with highwaymen rife on Putney Heath and the surrounding areas in the eighteenth century, and in particular, a local villain, Jerry Abershaw, who was caught and hung in 1795. Brandwood and Jephcote concluded their entry on the pub with the story that Mr Abershaw's last wish was to be hung without his boots on, to spite his mother's prediction he'd die with his shoes on!

THE MALTESE CAT

Aubyn Square, SW15 5NT

Opened on 1 December 1961, this was another post-war Young's pub. It was designed by Stuart Archer(who was also behind the Castle in Battersea) and who received the George Cross for his bravery during the Second World War.

The distinctive name came from the Rudyard Kipling book of the same name about a polo pony, the local link being the fact the pub was located a short distance from the site of Roehampton's old polo ground. It was a fixture in the Nicholson pub guides of the 1980s and '90s which praised the pub for its floodlit patioed garden, while Martin Green in 1982 stated there was sometimes even entertainment from a 'strolling minstrel'.

Located on the Aubyn Square estate, it was tucked away just off Roehampton Lane, the main road through the area. This may have hindered its opportunity to attract passing trade and it had closed by 2005, being demolished for flats not long after.

MONTAGUE ARMS

3 Medfield Street, SW15 4JY

The last of our Roehampton trio and by far the oldest as it is thought to date back to the seventeenth century. It received a Grade II listing from English Heritage in 1983 but sadly closed for the last time in 2005.

Its listed status was completely ignored by the property company Carrington Sears which acquired it in late 2009 and set about gutting the interior with the intention of turning it into flats. Wandsworth Council stepped in, ordering the company to restore it to its original condition with the then leader Eddie Lister stating that the pub had been 'a central focal point in Roehampton for centuries'.

Its listed status is no doubt partly why the building remains standing today, and if passing by now, you could be forgiven for thinking a traditional pub has survived here with the signage at the top of the building remaining. Looking closer, it sadly reveals itself as a Lloyds Local Convenience Store but at least some of the character of the historic exterior has been retained, something that looked in jeopardy at the start of the last decade.

THE ORIGINAL WOODMAN

42–44 Battersea High Street, SW11 3HX

Now from time to time in London you get pubs with the same name fairly near each other (the Blue Posts in Soho or the Red Lions near Green Park spring to mind) but two pubs on the same road with virtually the same name (the other being simply called The Woodman) only separated by half a dozen buildings must surely have been a one off.

Despite this being called 'Original', the other Woodman came first. The *South London Press* did a feature on both pubs in 1983, interviewing the respective landlords who maintained that their pubs served different clienteles, and both rubbed along perfectly well without trying to poach each other's customers! There was also a little bit of humour between the two pubs in the shape of their inn signs. The Woodman's showed a wood cutter while the Original had a beaver who'd gnawed away at a tree, which in effect would be an original woodman before men with axes came along.

The Original Woodman closed down in 2003 and metamorphosed into the Le QuecumBar jazz bar, self-styled as London's World Premier Gypsy Swing Jazz Venue. Sadly, this too is no more, managing to survive the covid lockdowns but sadly not a dispute with the landlord of the building over a new lease, and the future of the building remains uncertain.

THE PLOUGH

518 Wandsworth Road, SW8 3JX

This pub once served as the tap room of the Plough Brewery located next door but ended up far outlasting the brewery from which it took its name. The brewery shut down way back in 1935 and was converted into offices.

The pub ownership split away from the brewery in 1923/4 when it was acquired by the Wandsworth institution Young's. They then ran the place for the best part of ninety years until it was sold in the early 2010s, becoming a cocktail bar called Mist on Rocks and leased by the company which had operated the bar/club The Artesian Well based across the road, which closed in 2014 due to persistent complaints from residents about anti-social behaviour. I did pop into The Plough a couple of times just before the transition and it seemed like a pre-drinking venue for The Well by this point, which seemed a little out of keeping with the then traditional interior.

The Mist didn't last long before this too closed in 2017. The ground floor is due to be converted into a coffee shop; at the time of writing it remains unoccupied but thankfully the impressive façade has been retained.

THE RAVEN

140 Westbridge Road, SW11 5PF

The Raven was one of Battersea's most historic pubs and was built in the late seventeenth century. Apparently, it was even frequented by royalty, and supposedly Charles II was a regular visitor. The story goes that there were also secret passageways underneath the building. It began life as a coaching inn with comments online suggesting that as late as the 1950s the back area was still laid out as a stable. It was Grade II listed in 1951 and thirteen years later assumed the mantle of Battersea's oldest pub as the original Castle was demolished further down the High Street.

When it featured in the *Romance of Thame-Side Taverns* in 1969, Glyn Morgan drew particular attention to the heated foot rail around the bar which he said was the only one of its kind in London. It's certainly not anything I've encountered on my travels, although I think it would be a particularly nifty innovation during the winter months.

The Raven was included in the 1999 *Time Out* guide which called it a 'tranquil pub' with 'low ceiling and dark timbers'.

Just over a decade later it closed for good and reopened as Melanzana, an Italian restaurant I visited multiple times in 2018/19, at the time having no idea of the rich history of the pub that preceded it.

THE WHITE LION

14–16 High Street, SW11 1SL

This imposing former pub on Putney High Street still looms large over the area, despite having been derelict for several years. The present building dates from 1887 with records suggesting there had been an inn of this name in Putney as far back as 1636.

In a paper for the Wandsworth Historical Society focused on Putney's pubs, Dorian Gerhold suggested that the stone lion at the top of the current building had been taken from its seventeenth century predecessor. He also referenced the fact that in 1895 the White Lion was said to have 'magnificent' American bowling and skittles saloons.

By the latter part of the twentieth century it was home to a different type of entertainment as it played host to several gigs for artists starting to establish themselves across the post-punk and new wave genres. This included names such as Gary Numan and X Ray Spec, with an entire concert of the latter from 1977 here that can be enjoyed via the delights of YouTube. The building received Grade II listing in 1983.

In 1990 it appeared in the *Nicholson London Pub Guide* where its tie collection was flagged as a key item of interest! Four years later it was all change, the Lion was out and the Slug (and Lettuce) in as it became a part of that growing chain of pubs. We can only assume the ties were disposed of in the process.

The noughties rolled it through a series of chain bar identities like The Littern Tree and Walkabout. Its final persona was the bar Wahoo. This closed back in 2015 and the building has sat derelict ever since, which seems curious given how busy Putney High Street is. Meanwhile The Lion still looks down on the busy road while the dark branding of Wahoo that has weathered with time doesn't show this impressive building in its best light.

CAMDEN

THE BLACK CAP

171 Camden High Street, NW1 7JY

A landmark pub on the London drag scene, a pub called the Black Cap had been located in Camden since the 1750s, taking its name from a local witch as the full name was originally the Mother Black Cap.

It was during the mid-1960s when the drag shows first started here, replacing the Irish ceilidh music which had been the main source of live entertainment. Star of the show from this period until his death in 1983 was Rex Jameson, whose drag persona was called Mrs Shufflewick. Big names to grace the pub over the years included Danny Le Rue and Paul O'Grady during his time as Lily Savage.

By the 1990s it was being called the London palladium of late-night drag by the *Evening Standard,* mentioning the mixture of acts from singers to comedians, or as their writer put it 'formidable dames not to be crossed'. The upstairs bar had been renamed Shufflewicks in Rex's honour. Its review in the 1999 *Time Out* guide called it both 'pleasant' and 'ambient', noting its décor style as 'a brilliantly coloured hotel lounge', although adding that the 'carpet may require some to wear sunglasses'.

All was well at the Black Cap until the early 2010s when owners Faucet Inn (a name I'm sure one of the performers here would have had plenty of fun with) revealed their plans to redevelop the upper floors into residential accommodation. Given the lively nature of the pub, many were fearful noise complaints would snuff out the venue.

It was initially assigned ACV status in 2013, something the owners successfully overturned. The plans for the upper floors were rejected by Camden Council in February 2015. A new ACV was applied to the pub two months later yet barely a week later Faucet pulled down the shutters. The theory at the time was that it would be harder to get the ACV status to stick if it was no longer a going concern.

New owners purchased the building in 2021 and told the *Camden New Journal* they had high hopes of reopening the Black Cap. At the time of writing the pub remains closed but there remains an active campaign group trying to get the music playing and the lights shining again.

THE BREE LOUISE

69 Coburg Street, NW1 2HH

This well-loved Euston pub ended up becoming one of the unlikely symbols of the battle that raged over the mega transport project HS2. It first opened in 1827 as the Jolly Gardeners, a name it retained until 2004 when the then new owners Craig and Karen Douglas renamed it after their daughter who had died at only twelve weeks old.

Under the Douglases' stewardship the Bree became a beacon for beer lovers and the selection available in the pub often resembled a small beer festival rather than a backstreet pub in NW1 with well over fifteen different ales regularly available. The place thrived both with travellers grabbing a quick pint (or three) before jumping on the train at Euston as well as students from nearby UCL, the group I fell into when first discovering the Bree in 2007.

However, in 2012 the pub found itself within the red line boundary for the HS2 redevelopment. The Douglases fought hard to save the pub, taking their battle to Parliament and appearing in front of committee enquiries. Even during this period of uncertainty the Bree still kept picking up accolades and was named CAMRA's pub of the year 2016/17. The battle was ultimately and sadly in vain, and the pub closed its doors for the last time at the end of January 2018 and was rammed to the rafters over its final weekend.

The pub then stood empty until demolition took place at the end of June 2019. Doubts then surfaced on multiple occasions as to whether HS2 would ever reach Euston, with that phase of the project delayed for two years in spring 2023. It was then threatened with the axe before being confirmed in Rishi Sunak's 2023 party conference speech, albeit requiring private finance for completion and scaled back to the extent that the building will no longer extend to the site of the Bree, meaning it was demolished for nothing. Given how many twists and turns the saga has had, that may yet change, but at the time of writing it is certainly a galling situation.

THE CAMDEN FALCON

234 Royal College Street, NW1 9NJ

First landed on the scene in the mid-1850s as the Falcon, it hit new heights during the 1980s and '90s when it became known as one of the key live music pubs on the Camden scene. Pulp played there early in their career in 1988 and the story goes that Blur got signed to their first record deal based on one gig at The Falcon. Other acts that played here in the nineties included P.J. Harvey, Suede, The Verve and Coldplay in 1998 just before their assent to stardom.

In the same year it featured in the first *Time Out* pub guide, which summed the pub up by saying looking at it from the outside might make you think you'd 'need to take out medical insurance' to visit but once you got inside you'd be greeted by 'a dingy but friendly dive' full of indie types here for the music.

The Camden Falcon, by this time operating under the name Bar Fly, closed for good in 2002. The Bar Fly name was carried over to another venue closer to Chalk Farm tube while this building was converted into flats in 2010, although the old signage remained up for several years after closure.

THE CROWN AND GOOSE

100 Arlington Road, NW1 7HP

With roots back in the mid-1840s when it was simply known as The Crown Beer Shop, it only formally made the step up to being a fully licensed pub in the 1950s.

In the early nineties it had 'Goose' added to its name and soon after became known as one of the first gastropubs in the Camden area. When it appeared in the *Time Out* guide from 2005 the reviewer called it a 'regal-looking gastropub' and even suggested due to its ornate mirrors and banqueting hall lighting, it might be more at home in Primrose Hill.

It was around this period when the Goose found itself in a battle with developers who wanted to redevelop the site for housing. Permission for its demolition was initially given in 2008 but three years later this lapsed and a follow up application was rejected. Regrettably this proved to be a false dawn as in 2013 the pub confirmed they'd lost the battle and would be closing within months. The campaign to save the Goose included Camden royalty like Suggs from Madness, who said he was devastated it was closing and that it held a very special place in the heart of the community, adding that many of Madness's successful moments had been celebrated here.

The Crown and Goose was demolished the following year with a new block erected in its place, with the chain restaurant Turtle Bay occupying the ground floor.

THE HANSLER ARMS

133 King's Cross Road, WC1X 9BJ

This pint-sized pub in the shadow of King's Cross first opened in 1864. Its distinctive name came from a local man from the nineteenth century, Joseph Hansler, a Scandinavian diplomat who later became a British citizen and was the first man knighted by Queen Victoria.

The landlord here for a decade from 1979 was Mick McDuignan, who now runs the Sutton Arms in Clerkenwell with his son. In an article from early 2023, Mick reminisced about his time at the pub, including its popularity with the boys and girls in blue from the nearby King's Cross police station. He also recalled its popularity with another group in blue, Scottish football fans, who would descend *en masse* during the era of the Home Championship, a football tournament contested between the four nations of the United Kingdom.

In 1996 Peter Haydon called it a hidden gem and noted the pub was so cramped for space that they had to put the pictures on the ceiling as well as the walls. Roger Protz's review from the end of the eighties referenced old Punch cartoons and Victorian prints decorating the walls and the fact that once you got inside the pub, you could easily feel like you'd been transported to a rural ale house rather than being right by the hustle and bustle of King's Cross.

It closed in 2001 and became a Chinese restaurant called Bamboo which has also since closed.

THE HORSE AND GROOM

68 Heath Street, NW3 1DN

First trotted onto the Hampstead scene in the eighteenth century, in its early days this pub could count the painter George Romney as one of its regulars. The present building dates from 1899.

When reviewing the pub in 1982, Martin Green was very impressed by the fact that the chairman of Young's (who owned the pub) had visited to wish a happy birthday to the licensee, who was a woman in her 90s!

It popped up in several *Time Out* guides around the turn of the millennium with a constant in each review being a reference to carp in a fish tank on the bar. The review from 1998 was the most positive, in which it was referred to as 'an ideal bolt hole after heavy Hampstead shopping'.

It was Grade II listed in 1999 with the listing referring to its red brick and portland stone bands, as well as its tiled gabled roof and chimney stacks. As noted in a guide to Young's pubs from 1991, it looks very similar architecturally to The Orange Tree by Richmond station.

The pub had closed by the mid-noughties and the ground floor of the building has since been occupied by a restaurant, a letting agent and most recently has been converted into a skin care clinic. The gold Horse and Groom signage remains above the building's first floor windows.

THE KING OF BOHEMIA

10 Hampstead High Street, NW3 1PY

With lineage way back to the reign of Charles II, the King of Bohemia was originally located in front of the old Hampstead brewery. That closed in 1931 and the Bohemia was rebuilt four years later.

The Nicholson guide from 1987 gave the pub a thumbs up, referring to nice old photos of Hampstead on the wall and calling it a 'cheeky and relaxing' place. It featured in the first few *Evening Standard* guides which described it as 'smart and glossy'. However by the late 1990s the mood had turned and *Time Out* were not impressed by the Bohemia, describing it as having 'absolutely no class' and moaning about a soundtrack of 'over-loud boy bands' and noting it was only a nudge away from being as bad as a theme pub.

The King was dethroned in 2005 and has now been replaced by the clothes shop Reiss.

THE LILLIE LANGTRY

121 Abbey Road, NW6 4SL

First opened in 1969 on the ground floor of Emminster House, part of the new Abbey Road estate and replacing a previous pub called the Princess of Wales Hotel which had stood on the same site. The pub was named after Edward VII's mistress because of her supposed links to the area, and a street in the nearby Alexandra Estate completed in 1978 was also named after Langtry.

These local links were debunked by two historians in the *Camden New Journal* in May 2021, with the story said to originate from a last ditch bid to save Leighton House from demolition as part of the development of these estates by claiming Langtry had lived there. They instead contend Langtry lived in west London, where a pub near West Brompton still stands named after the actress and royal favourite. The pub also had a brief stint as the Cricketers in the late noughties but quickly reverted to its original moniker.

It was a new round of widespread redevelopment that ultimately did for the Lillie as the pub closed in September 2022 as Emminster House was earmarked for demolition as part of a wider estate regeneration plan from Camden Council. A month later it was featured in a piece in *The Guardian* looking at five pubs across England that had recently closed their doors. Interviews in the article suggested the pub had a bit of a rough reputation, with a former landlady calling it the 'roughest pub in Kilburn' but equally that it was well loved by the local community. This was well summed up by a quote from a regular, Mary O'Brien, a pensioner who'd been visiting the pub since its early days in the 1970s and who said it had been like a sanctuary to her against feelings of isolation and loneliness.

THE TALLY HO

9 Fortess Road, NW5 1AA

First opened in 1843, in the 1960s The Tally Ho become a key venue on the London jazz scene. The CAMRA *Whatpub* entry about here recalled that the Sunday lunchtime jam sessions were so popular that rows of pints would be pre-poured in anticipation for the opening rush!

A *Financial Times* article from 2020 about Camden and Kentish Town's musical legacies called The Tally Ho the 'ground zero of pub rock, which included Dr Feelgood, Ian Dury and Nick Lowe' during the 1970s. This was due to the pub's initial decision to let an American band called Eggs Over Easy play a residency here while they were recording nearby, which saw other musicians come to watch and then follow in their footsteps. In time this pub rock morphed into punk rock as the decade went on.

The final online reviews were a mixed bag, with some saying a classic pub had become a bit of a dive, with live music replaced by large screens for sports. Others felt people were being harsh and while the pub was a bit worn around the edges it was still a decent watering hole.

A planning application for the pub to be demolished and replaced by flats was first submitted in October 2004 and was approved by Camden Council; the pub closed at the end of the following year and demolition took place in autumn 2006.

THE VICTORIA

2 Mornington Crescent, NW1 7QD

Dating from the early reign of the monarch it was named after, this pub established itself as a backstreet boozer away from the hustle and bustle of Camden High Street.

It featured in the Nicholson guide in 1990 which praised the pub's garden and mentioned that barbecues took place there over the summer. Online reviews of the pub from the early 2000s include several celeb spots, with separate postings mentioning Rhys Ifans and Sean Bean and another Kate Moss and the Gallaghers (not together!). It also popped up in the film *Cassandra's Dream* from 2007, directed by Woody Allen and starring Ewan McGregor and Colin Farrell.

It closed abruptly in the summer of 2013, with the owner for the past thirteen years Christopher Barnes saying it was no longer viable to run as a business and seeking permission for a residential conversion. There was a concerted effort to try and save it but the plans eventually went through.

It was remembered fondly by BBC Radio London host Robert Elms in his book *London Made Us*, when he recalled how all the disparate elements of the local community used to come together here, juxtaposing the contrast between Kate Moss on one hand and posties from the local sorting office on another. But above all that, he lamented losing what he described as 'our' pub, something that will chime with anyone who has seen a favourite pub vanish before their eyes.

ISLINGTON

THE ALBERT/THE CHARLES LAMB

16 Elia Street, N1 8DE

A cosy corner pub, The Charles Lamb was a stone's throw away from the busy Upper Street thoroughfare and Angel tube station.

It opened as The Albert in 1839, the same year as Queen Victoria proposed to Prince Albert, and was known as that for much of its life. It was renamed in the mid-noughties after the local author Charles Lamb, who used Elia (the street this pub was on) as one of his pen names.

Writing on the name change in his book on Clerkenwell and Islington pubs published in 2016, Johnny Homer remarked it is a shame whenever such a longstanding name is altered but it is more palatable if it has some local links to it, a position I'm very sympathetic to.

I visited here a few times between 2016 to 2018 and I always found it a peaceful haven away from the crowds of the main drag, and reasonably priced too. The pub reopened in 2020 post the initial covid lockdown but did not re-emerge in 2021.

THE COPENHAGEN

283 Camden Road, N7 0JN

Dating from 1965, the Copenhagen served as a replacement for another pub of the same name which had been located on York Road/Way from the early nineteenth century until the 1940s.

In 1980 it was described in a local Islington newspaper as having a quite pleasant patio but that the effect was diminished by the pub's position on the Camden Road. They went on to sum up the clientele as 'youngish disco types knocking back lager like there was no tomorrow' before adding philosophically, 'of course, there might not be'.

There was a major change at the pub in 2008 when it was acquired by Colombian owners who renamed it as the Latin Corner. It reverted to the original name five years later but shortly after the owners announced plans to demolish the pub and replace it with flats and a Sainsbury's Local. The pub's manager Linda Evans commented to the local newspaper she was gutted by the news and 500 people signed a petition opposing the closure in just ten days.

The pub had closed by that summer and briefly hosted a bookshop giving away free books. Initial applications to demolish the building were refused but this finally took place in 2018.

THE HAT AND FEATHERS

2 Clerkenwell Road, EC1M 5PQ

Here we have a lost pub which briefly reopened in the noughties after a long period of closure but its resurrection proved to be short lived. A Hat and Feathers first popped up here in the 1780s with the present building dating from the start of the 1860s. It was Grade II listed by English Heritage in 1981 before closing its doors by the end of the decade.

After this long period out in the cold it reopened in late 2006 and went straight into the next *Time Out* guide. The review was gushing about the restoration job done on the pub's interior, noting the etched windows and wood panelling as well as atmospheric gas lighting and gold leaf on the cornicing. The entry noted it as having some of the fanciest pub food around, like Gressingham Duck Risotto!

Sadly its second coming proved to be short-lived and in 2011 it closed again. The upper floors are being incorporated into the Hotel Indigo next door. There was talk of the ground floor becoming a restaurant but it was still unoccupied at the time of writing.

THE LAMB

46 North Road, N7 9DP

There were originally four pubs serving Caledonian Market. The market is long gone, as are all the pubs. The Lamb survived the longest.

The pub first opened in 1855, designed by John Bunstone Bunning who was also responsible for the market building. The market was a commercial failure and spent its latter days as a flea market before finally closing in 1963 and then being demolished, to be replaced by housing as well as Caledonian Park itself.

The Lamb was Grade II listed in 1972. In the text of the designation, the interior was noted as still having a nineteenth century bar front as well as fragments of the original decoration with a frieze on two sides of the bar.

While the other pubs which served the market had all closed by the mid-1980s, The Lamb persevered into the new millennium. It shut its doors for good in 2004. The upper floors were converted into flats but according to a CAMRA listing of the building from 2021, the ground floor remained capable of being reopened as a pub should anyone wish to take the plunge.

NEW MERLIN'S CAVE

34 Margery Street, WC1X 0JJ

Built in the early 1920s, this replaced two other pubs also called Merlin's Cave which had been situated nearby.

When a licence for live music to be performed here was granted by the LCC shortly after opening, the wording stated that the pub could host 'musical entertainment to which customers sitting around tables may contribute, if they feel so inclined'. The book *Taverns around Town* from 1937 gave the musical entertainment a thumbs up, referring to 'well conducted cabaret shows' running on various nights a week.

By the 1960s the musical theme had switched to jazz and it was described by Martin Green as a 'mecca for mainstream trad-jazz enthusiasts'. By the start of the 1990s, it was still highly rated as a jazz pub. In his book on London pubs, David Gammell stated it attracted customers across all ages and backgrounds, united by a love of jazz. On Wednesdays to Saturdays the music would go on beyond midnight.

The music did not go on beyond the mid-nineties as the Cave closed in 1994 and was demolished for flats by the end of the decade. These have at least been called Merlin Court in a nod to the past.

THE OLD PARR'S HEAD

66 Cross Street, N1 2BA

Another pub with a fine historical legacy, the present building dates from the early nineteenth century but an earlier iteration of the pub played host to a key performance.

In the eighteenth century there were theatrical shows put on at the Parr and it was here that John Henderson recited Thomas Garrick's *Ode to Shakespeare*, showing the long history of pubs and theatre in Angel which is continued to this day with The Old Red Lion.

The Parr in question, Thomas, reputedly lived to the ripe old age of 122 through the fifteenth to seventeenth centuries. He first came to prominence in 1635 after a pamphlet of his life was written by John Taylor, better known as the Water Poet. The Parr outlived its namesake and made it well into its third century. It appeared in Hardens' 2003 pub guide where it was described as a very pleasant mix of styles between old and new.

The pub closed three years later and was converted into a branch of the Jigsaw clothes shop and is now a Monsoon. The pub's distinctive orange tiled frontage has been retained.

SIR GEORGE ROBEY

240 Seven Sisters Road, N4 2HX

This originally opened as The Clarence Hotel. It wasn't until the end of the 1960s when it was rechristened as the Sir George Robey, the name coming from a music hall star who frequently performed at the Rainbow Theatre opposite the pub. Initially the pub's theme reflected the musical hall connection with various bits of memorabilia decorating the walls. In 1982 Martin Green reflected that these decorations meant it was a rare example of a theme pub that actually worked.

By the end of the decade it had become a live music haunt, with something on every night of the week. While initially there had been a tendency towards Irish and folk music, the repertoire expanded into the 1990s with punk and rock shows. Huge names to play here included Blur in their early days and Hawkwind. It also established a reputation as a buzzing late venue, turning into a club on Fridays and

Saturdays which stayed open until 6am, although apparently it was soft drinks only after 2am. When it featured in *Evening Standard* guides during the mid-1990s, Angus McGill noted that someone told him they'd get 300 ravers here on weekends.

During this same period north London author Nick Hornby paid homage to the pub in his 1995 book *High Fidelity*. Hornby used it as the inspiration for the fictitious Harry Lauder pub frequented by the book's main character. Harry Lauder was also a star of musical hall, albeit a hundred years earlier than Robey.

In 1996 it was acquired by Vince Power who ran the Mean Fiddler group, and who moved his music venue Powerhaus here from Angel, renaming The Robey accordingly. The Powerhaus then hosted German hard rockers Rammstein's first ever UK gig the following year.

The lights went off at the Powerhaus in 2004 when Power split from the Mean Fiddler group and went it alone with his own set of venues, not choosing to retain this as one of them. The next year it was purchased by the incredibly rock and roll sounding Consistent Management Solutions Limited. They unveiled bold plans to turn The Robey into a thriving hub of activity including a bar, casino and music venue.

It turns out the new owners failed to live up to their name as they couldn't put their solution into effect. The building then lay derelict yet defiant for over ten years until it was demolished for housing in 2015.

WHITE CONDUIT HOUSE

14 Barnsbury Road, N1 0HB

This pub took its name from a celebrated tearoom on this site from the seventeenth century. This backed onto an expansive garden with a fishpond and was a popular retreat for those wishing to escape the city. The tea rooms were mentioned by writers of the age such as Oliver Goldsmith and George Cruickshank. The original house was demolished in 1849 with the pub put in its place a few years later.

In the 1990s the pub was renamed the Penny Farthing, which caused significant disquiet from residents in the local media, given the historic link the original name had to the tea house and pleasure gardens. In happier news it was also Grade II listed in this decade, gaining the status in 1994.

The Farthing lasted until the mid-noughties when it closed and was initially converted into an Italian restaurant. It has since gone through a few different owners and is now presently Little Georgia, part of a very small chain of restaurants serving up Caucasian food. The White Conduit House lettering can be seen at the very top of the building.

TOWER HAMLETS

BLACK HORSE/THE HOUSE THEY LEFT BEHIND

27 Ropemaker's Fields, E14 8BX

This began life as The Black Horse which first opened in 1807 and was then rebuilt in 1857. It survived the blitz, although the buildings on either side sustained damage. They were eventually demolished in the 1960s which left the pub as the last building standing, which led to it acquiring the name of The House They Left Behind. For a long time it was isolated on its own before new flats were eventually built adjacent to it.

It made regular appearances in pub guides in the 1990s. Peter Haydon noted that the pub did a roaring trade in liver and bacon (despite the fact the landlady didn't enjoy making it) which also attracted the attention of Max, the German Shepherd from The Grapes across the road in its pre-Gandalf era. Hopefully the bacon kept him away from the resident ginger cat mentioned in the Nicholson guide entry.

Time Out's review from 1998 referred to it as the landlord Tony's 'personal funhouse', with a décor they described as 'East End dabbles with ancient Greece', as well as mentioning the fact he had his 'wedding jacket framed on the wall'. By this point the liver and bacon had been replaced by Tex Mex.

In its last years it was rebranded as The House, a modern high end English restaurant and then two further restaurants, X UNDERS and finally Melaka before closing and being converted into housing in 2009.

CITY PRIDE

1 West Ferry Road, E14 8JH

This pub was built in the 1950s for the dockers, but it was able to adapt in the 1980s and '90s as the area changed beyond recognition with the Canary Wharf and wider Docklands developments.

On its own website in the early 2000s it referred to itself as one of the only traditional pubs left in the Docklands and a great escape for drinking, dining and relaxing. The pub was also used by the BBC as a filming spot for the London Marathon.

It made the papers in 2008 when it was sold for an eye-watering £32 million to developers who planned to redevelop the site with a massive sixty storey tower comprised of hotels and apartments, taking advantage of its location near Canary Wharf.

A story in the *Daily Mirror* carried a quote from a disgruntled regular of the pub who said he was sick of decent pubs closing to be replaced by posh hotels and fancy gastropubs, adding he just wanted somewhere for a pint, peanuts and pork scratchings.

The City Pride was demolished in 2012. In the end the tower built here was seventy-five storeys high and was named after the pub it usurped. I think if you'd been drinking here back in the 1970s and suggested one day it would be replaced by a skyscraper apartment block, the regulars would think you were definitely one over the eight.

FIVE BELLS & BLADEBONE

27 Three Colt Street, E14 8HH

Located near the former West India Docks, the pub was originally simply called the Five Bells when it first opened in 1806. This was a reference to the signal that would be given to dockers to return to work. There are two stories as to where the Bladebone bit came from. One theory contended that it was added to the name in 1845 after the discovery of razor-sharp knives on the site of an abattoir nearby. The other, which was referenced in H.E. Popham's 1937 book *The Taverns in the Town,* was that a whale's bladebone used to hang outside the pub. Popham recounts that it was removed in the early twentieth century and taken to the headquarters of the Taylor Walker brewery which owned the pub and put on display there, puzzling visitors!

Unsurprisingly the pub was full of naval memorabilia, with a ship's wheel built into a partition wall, artefacts from various vessels, pictures of tea clippers and other boats decorating the walls and even a Toby jug of Lord Nelson. In J.P. Hughes' book on East End pubs from 2000 he referred to a python in its tank which was by the bar! The same book also mentioned a spectacular hanging brass lamp holder, I am impressed he was still able to focus on ornamental light fittings despite the jeopardy of a large snake on a tank.

In its final days it was renamed for the new millennium as the 5B Urban Bar, and as the photo overleaf demonstrates, an exterior that looked like it had been decorated by Laurence Llewelyn-Bowen. This lasted nearly twenty years before closing in 2018.

URBAN
BAR
5b
GREAT FOOD
URBAN
BAR
5b
Havana Club
5b URBAN BAR

GRAVE MAURICE

269 Whitechapel Road, E1 1BY

Another pub very much established in East End lore, the Maurice was rebuilt in 1874, having first opened way back in 1723.

In the 1950s and '60s it was a favoured haunt of the Kray brothers, and Ronnie was even interviewed here for a TV show. According to a website about the duo, he played to the audience in this appearance, dressed up like Al Capone with a fitted coat going right down to his ankles. The same website also states that he would sit at the bar so he had a clear view of whoever entered the pub.

For forty years the pub was run by a woman called Christina who was by all accounts very eccentric. An evening manager of the pub during the 1980s and '90s recalled online how she did her own butchering in the cellar, often having a half cow delivered down the trapdoor. He described how the pub at this point was largely unaltered since the 1950s with a plush interior, only playing classical music during the day and jazz at night.

In 1995 everyone's favourite outspoken vegetarian Morrissey was photographed outside the pub for the cover of his Under the Influence compilation album, thankfully Christina having moved on by now. This would have led to an interesting meeting of groups in the late '90s as it is unclear how much crossover there is between Morrissey fans and those who enjoy visiting the haunts of East End gangsters of days gone by.

In its final years it suffered the ignominy of being modernised into a dull modern bar, renamed as The Q Bar at the Grave Maurice in 2004. Six years later Maurice had both feet in the grave as the pub shut and was converted into a betting shop.

LORD RODNEY'S HEAD

285 Whitechapel Road, E1 1BY

This was a traditional East End boozer located next to the hustle and bustle of Whitechapel Market. The current building dates from 1885 with the pub itself thought to have roots back to the early nineteenth century.

Ted Bruning praised the pub in his 2001 book *Historic Pubs of London* for its East End authenticity, saying 'If you want to step straight into the past, don't miss it!', noting its wooden floorboards as well as old rickety chairs and as the basic food offering of a handful of cheese rolls under a glass dome on the bar. The pub's clock collection also caught the eye as Bruning estimated there were over 100 lining the picture rail shelf.

In the earlier noughties the pub changed hands and was renamed and modernised as the Funky Munky in a 'bizarre scrapyard style'. This only lasted five years before the place closed down completely.

NEEDLE GUN/THE TRADER

527 Roman Road, E3 5EL

Thought to date back to the early 1870s (although the building itself is from 1827), the pub got a direct hit on the first night of the blitz but was rebuilt and reopened after the war.

Testimony from a Tower Hamlets local history project remembered this as being a proper East End pub back in the day, with piano sing songs taking place regularly. The pub's darts team was also very active in the local pub leagues.

In 2000 J.P. Hughes wrote that it had probably the nicest pub garden in Tower Hamlets, thanks to its trees, bushes and roses making it a delightful place on summer days, as well as having an interior decorated with photos from anything from Monet to the Muppets.

It was renamed The Trader in 2005 before closing completely in 2009 and being converted into a budget hotel. The present grey exterior seems in sharp contrast to when it used to be 'ablaze with flowers' in the summer during its pub days.

THE NORTH POLE

74 Manilla Street, E14 8LG

Dating back to the 1860s, this was one of the last survivors of a previous age on the Isle of Dogs before the rampant change of the 1980s and '90s associated with the development of Canary Wharf.

The *Evening Standard* raved about it in a review from 2009 where they called it a 'top local' with a friendly welcoming atmosphere which made it 'an excellent alternative to the unimaginative boredom' of the areas by the waterfront.

The writer also showed a degree of foresight when predicting the area around the pub was due for massive redevelopment, something they hoped wouldn't affect the pub anytime soon. Well it wasn't too much later when the pub closed in 2014 with the buildings around it for the chop.

On this occasion the developers stated the pub would be retained and in due course reopen. The spiel on their website from January 2020 claimed the pub would be refurbished and then reopen its 'iconic green doors' (can't beat the use of the word iconic on a property website) to be the crowning gem of the new development which is latterly referred to in the same piece as a 'vertical village'.

Vertical, horizontal or lopsided, this new 'village' is still missing its pub as the 'iconic' doors remain closed. Let's hope for iconic drinks, snacks and chat to flow here again in the near future.

THE RESOLUTE

210 Poplar High Street, E14 0BB

The Resolute opened in 1937, replacing a pub of the same name which had stood here since the mid-nineteenth century and was originally called The Harrow.

In 2000 J.P. Hughes referred to it as a beautiful pub 'both inside and out'; features he highlighted included the little panels of stained glass above the bar, upholstered bench seating and the hanging lamps which lit the place.

James Watson, CAMRA's pub protection officer for Hackney, had this as his local before he moved up to north London and he raved to me about the pub and its Art Deco style interior.

It wasn't just the design of the pub he loved, to him the pub embodied a cracking community spirit. He was here having a drink on the evening after the

7/7 terrorist attacks. The news was on in the pub and the head of the Metropolitan Police came on, saying all the things you'd expect about vigilance and everyone going on with their daily lives, he then said everyone needed to be resolute. At that point the landlord rang the bell to say 'Did you hear? He said we need to stay at The Resolute, happy hour everyone!' In a moment where so many people would have been worried about loved ones and worried about potential follow up attacks, the pub again proved to be somewhere for the community to rally round and get through it all, together.

The pub closed in 2011 and was demolished in rather rapid order to be replaced with a generic block of flats.

TOLLESBURY BARGE

Millwall Inner Dock, E14 9SL

While its stint as a pub was relatively short, The Tollesbury had an eventful time during its life as an operational barge. It was built in 1901 and played its part in the Dunkirk evacuation of June 1940 in the Second World War, bringing back around 270 men to Britain and surviving the onslaught from enemy planes above.

By the 1990s it had become a pub (although it was initially referred to as the Tollesbury Wine Barge) in the Docklands. It was damaged by the IRA bomb in the area in February 1996. In their review from 2002, *Time Out* stated it was popular as an afterwork hangout for a predominantly young couple crowd. They also mentioned there was Harvey's Best on tap, something certainly worth mooring up for.

All was happy on board until September 2005 when the barge sank! It was thankfully rescued and shifted to a mooring in Barking. Six years later it was bought and restored into a houseboat, having also served this purpose in the 1970s.

In 2021 it featured in an extended article on the American website *Newsweek,* written by Rachael Smith who restored the boat with her partner Euan Maybank.

THE WATER POET

9–11 Folgate Street, E1 6BX

Although its lifespan was very brief in comparison to others featured in this book, the Water Poet still managed to leave its mark on Londoners in that time.

There had been a pub on this site going back to the late eighteenth century called the Pewter Plate, but by the 1970s the premises had been converted into offices. It was revived as a pub during the nineties and took its name from the fact the owner John Taylor shared his with a historical figure from Spitalfields' past who

had the nickname of the Water Poet. Avid readers will recall his connection to The Old Parr's Head earlier on in the book.

This sprawling six room pub soon became a hit with Londoners. In its appearance in the *Time Out* guide from 1999, the review stated it was 'open, airy and minimalist' but 'a far cry from the factory farmed vibe of All Bar One' and other chains. In the mid-noughties it briefly reverted to its original name before becoming the Water Poet once more.

One of its major selling points was its sizable beer garden, always a bonus for any central London pub. The pub also hosted a wide array of events from pancake races through to Eurovision parties.

The closure of the pub was announced in February 2019 with both *Londonist* and *Time Out* dedicating articles to the 'loss of a beloved boozer', with the doors closing for good on 29 March 2019. This was due to a wider redevelopment of the Norton Folgate area. These plans attracted a significant amount of criticism, including from the band Madness who had released an entire album about the area in 2009.

The Water Poet continues to live on in people's affections, as evidenced by its appearance in a 2023 *Londonist* article asking readers to choose one London venue they wanted to bring back from the dead.

RICHMOND

THE CHARLIE BUTLER

40 Mortlake High Street, SW14 8HR

This was the only London pub named after a (then) living employee of the brewery that owned it. The man himself was an award-winning head horse keeper at Young's Brewery in nearby Wandsworth. It replaced an earlier pub on the site called Old George which had been demolished as part of a road widening project. It opened in 1968, two years after Butler had retired after forty-three years' service to the brewery. In his tenure with Young's their horses won over 3,000 first prizes and championships across various shows across England. Butler passed away in 1980.

The decision to dispense with the Old George name was not entirely popular with the locals, and a petition was organised that received over 100 signatures, calling for Young's to think again. This included a regular, Mr Charlie Blackburn, aged eighty-eight and a regular at the Old George since he'd been fourteen. Young's were not for turning and when the pub opened, Mr Blackburn popped in for the opening and was quizzed by reporters. He stated that both the new name and new pub would take some getting used to, but he acknowledged the beer was still just as good!

The pub was a stone's throw away from The Stag Brewery, owned by various companies over the years including Watneys and AB InBev (who produced Budweiser there) which is now derelict awaiting redevelopment.

In 2011 plans were brought forward for the demolition of the pub and its replacement with flats. A petition was set up to oppose the move and this was featured on the *London Jazz News* website in 2011 as the pub hosted open mic and jam sessions. The campaign was unsuccessful and the pub closed the following year. While it was waiting for the wrecking ball it was subject to a police raid in November 2012, where over 100 officers swarmed the building, finding Class A and B drugs.

The pub was demolished in 2013 but Charlie Butler's legacy lives on in a most unexpected location. The pub's sign is now on display (and featured in the photo above) in the Flying Saucer Draught Emporium in Houston, Texas. It has been on display there since the bar first opened in 2000. The founder of the Saucer, Keith Schlabs, was friends with John and James Young, who gifted him ten of their pub signs at the turn of the millennium when the brewery was doing a refresh across their pub estate. You wonder how many Texans enjoying a beer at the Emporium have glanced up at the sign and wondered who Charlie Butler was!

THE HAM BREWERY TAP

4–6 Ham Street, TW10 7HT

The pub first opened in 1893 and was rebuilt in 1934 as the building which now stands today. The pub's usual white exterior was temporarily repainted as a 'vile yellow' as a joke in 2003, before thankfully being reinstated to its more subdued theme.

In the 2010s, the pub was still going strong, the CAMRA website reporting that there were events there most nights, including poker, karaoke, quizzes and even Sunday meat auctions. The pub had closed by 2019 but their Twitter account still remains online, the last post being from August 2018 with a video of a group of men and women of all ages having a whale of a time dancing along to The Gap Band's 1979 hit *Oops Upside Your Head* with the disco lights in full swing.

In 2022 a planning application was submitted but then withdrawn for the site to be converted into a vet's surgery. It remains derelict at the time of writing.

THE HOLE IN THE WALL

3 Park Road, TW10 6NS

Beginning life as the Park Road Arms and thought to date from 1868, it was soon nicknamed the Hole in the Wall due to its small size, and renamed to reflect this in 1967 after being rebuilt by the brewery Ind Coope. The pub closed in 2006 and it was shortly after that when it found itself in the national newspaper following a macabre discovery.

Developers were soon eyeing up the closed pub as a prime spot for new flats. It just so happened that the next-door neighbour was none other than Sir David Attenborough and he bought the building in 2009 with the aim of preserving it by sympathetically incorporating it into his property while retaining the greenery of the pub garden.

While work was taking place the following year, workers discovered a skull buried in the earth. This was identified to be that of Julia Thomas, who lived approximately where Attenborough's house now stands and was murdered by her housekeeper, Kate Webster, in 1879 in a particularly gruesome manner, with her body being dismembered. The majority of what remained of Mrs Thomas was discovered washed up in the river soon after the crime occurred and Webster, who had fled to Ireland, was arrested, and hung that same year, the only woman to be executed at Wandsworth Prison.

THE MANOR ARMS

62 Railway Side, SW13 0PQ

A small but perfectly formed establishment, the Manor Arms was located down a small passageway in Barnes called Railway Side. Given how tucked away it was, if you didn't know it was there you could very easily miss it. It also had no road access whatsoever, so it must have been an interesting sight to see the delivery of barrels from the nearest road along the narrow alley.

In November 2011 it was renamed as the Idle Hour, which lasted for just over four years before the bell tolled for the last time at the start of February 2016. It wasn't long before the application came in to convert the building into a house and two flats. The work was soon completed but the pub's green tiled frontage has been retained alongside signage stating it is The Manor Arms.

QUEEN DOWAGER

49 North Lane, TW11 0HU

Thought to have begun its life as either the Two or Jolly Lawyers (certainly not a pub name you can imagine being popular these days), by 1851 it had been renamed the Queen Dowager in honour of William IV's widow, Queen Adelaide. It was an appropriately local connection as they'd both lived a few minutes away at Bushy House, which is now used by the National Physical Laboratory.

Talking of the Laboratory, the pub was mentioned as being popular with staff from that facility in Helen Osborn's second book on the Young's pub estate, *Young at Heart*. It was owned by the brewery from 1860 right through to its closure in October 2011. An article from the local news site *Teddington Town* said that the pub had gone through several landlords in the period running up to the closure and the final occupants were only given nine days' notice it would be closing down. The same report states the licensees Shaun and Kathryn wanted to go out with a

bang so they held a closing party with live music. The pub was demolished less than six months later and replaced by flats.

At the start of 2023 the pub sign for the Queen Dowager popped up on eBay, as part of a wider auction of old Young's pub signs.

THE TRIPLE CROWN

15 Kew Foot Road, TW9 2SS

Located at the end of the quaint Kew Foot Road, this was another hidden away boozer in Richmond. It was originally called The Tulip Tree and reportedly dates back to at least 1870, although the markings at the top of the building suggest it could be from 1884.

It was renamed The Triple Crown in 1985 by the then landlord, who was Irish, and wished to mark the fact his home country had achieved that honour in that year's Five Nations Tournament – for the uninitiated that is achieved by beating all the 'home nations' (so in Ireland's case England, Scotland and Wales). It also made sense for the pub to link in with Rugby given its proximity to Richmond Athletic Ground which is home to both Richmond and the London Scottish rugby teams.

In the 1990s it became known for having a wide range of ales on offer and regularly featured across multiple London pub guides. By the noughties the pub still came recommended but with the disclaimer the beer selection had narrowed somewhat.

Their archived website from 2016 claimed the pub was 'Richmond's Best Kept Secret' – it closed not too long after. At the time of writing there has been no residential conversion so while its future may remain uncertain, The Triple Crown could once again return to the Richmond pub scene.

THE THREE PIGEONS

87 Petersham Road, TW10 6UT

Originally dating from 1715 and located slightly further inland from the river, the pub was rebuilt on the riverside in 1871 following the intervention of the local landowner, the Duke of Buccleuch. The building was designed by John MacVicar Anderson, a future president of RIBA.

In the 1980s, the then owners put the cat amongst the pigeons by putting in place a partial rebranding as 'The Raj', with a theme styled on the rather questionable concept of the 'Thirties Spirit of English India'. This look featured pink walls, trellis arches and big plants everywhere. The menu was revamped to include Balti curries. The Raj idea did not go down well with the good folk of Richmond and the pub soon reverted to the good old Three Pigeons. Meanwhile 'The Raj' concept was tried again, this time at what was and thankfully is now again The Mitre in Holland Park.

In November 1993, the pub closed after bailiffs came in and seized items such as furniture and glassware and the electric supply was cut off. The place had become dilapidated, and the owners were embarking on a significant renovation when in March 1994 disaster struck. A fire broke out in mysterious circumstances, strongly suspected to have been started deliberately, which ripped through the building and caused half a million pounds worth of damage. The refurbishment work halted and the pub's future remained uncertain for many years. The last hope of the Pigeons returning as a pub was extinguished in the late 2000s when the building was converted into flats.

WATER GIPSIES

183 Ashburnham Road, TW10 7NR

A post-war pub opening in 1967 to serve the newly built Wates estate next door. It was named after a book of the same name by A.P. Herbert, which itself had featured a fictional inn based on the famous Hammersmith riverside pub, The Dove. His wife, Lady Herbert, provided the illustration for the pub's sign.

It quickly became popular and was referenced in a 1979 local newspaper report as 'not so much a pub, more a way of life', and the same article also spoke positively of the basket meals available there.

That way of life came to an end in 2003 when the pub closed and it was converted into a nursery two years later. An element of the Gipsies continued to live on though, as an online blogger discovered the pub's sign in a nearby front garden in 2014.

THE WHITE HART

70 High Street, TW12 2SW

This former pub can claim impressive literary and theatrical connections. Not only was it once owned by the actor David Garrick (who has a pub as well as a theatre named after him in Central London), it was also featured in a scene in *Oliver Twist* where Bill Sykes and Oliver stopped for drinks before a burglary in nearby Chertsey.

The pub was rebuilt in 1898 so the present building cannot directly claim these connections. It remained in business until 2003 before being converted into flats the next year.

OUTER SOUTH WEST (KINGSTON/MERTON/SUTTON)

THE BURN BULLOCK

315 London Road, CR4 4BE

This venerable old pub has a history going back hundreds of years but faces a distinctly uncertain future. The pub was called The Kings Arms when it first opened in the late sixteenth century, and some parts of the original building remain today.

It was Grade II listed in 1954. At the time it was run by the retired Surrey cricketer Burnett 'Burn' Bullock and his wife Lily. It seemed an appropriate spot for a former cricketer given its location right by Mitcham Cricket Club. Burnett died at the end of that same year but his widow stayed on as landlady until her own retirement in 1975. Shortly after Lily's departure the pub was renamed in honour of her late husband.

The Bullock continued at the crease until 2013 when it closed down and barely a year after this the poor state of the building led English Heritage to place it on their risk register. It was acquired by Phoenix Investments in 2016 who promised the restoration of the Bullock as part of a plan to turn the upper floors into flats.

These plans have not materialised, while the building's condition became ever more perilous with the car park being used at one stage as an unlicensed scrapyard. While the developers continued to state a restored pub was part of the plan for the site, there was still no progress on site and in April 2024 the building suffered significant damage in a major fire. Merton Council stated they recognised the desire for the restoration of the building but noted the challenges given the private ownership of the site.

THE CRICKETERS

340 London Road, CR4 3ND

Another cricket connection here. The pub is thought to have first opened in 1789, with records indicating it was briefly renamed as The White Swan at the start of the nineteenth century. It became a Young's pub in 1831.

The pub's cricket links weren't just in the name as it served both as a headquarters for the local club in Mitcham, including providing dressing room facilities for the players. The Australian cricket team also trained locally at the club during the early Ashes tours at the end of the nineteenth century.

The pub was destroyed by a bomb on 23 September 1940 during the blitz and then had a spell trading from a temporary hut until a replacement building was completed in late 1957, with an official opening ceremony on 9 January 1958. The first pints poured on this day were by the Surrey cricketing twins, Eric and Alec Bedser.

It was sold to property developers in 2009 who demolished it the following year and replaced it with flats. When the pub was being cleared in 2010, photos of local cricketers which had previously decorated the saloon bar were found in a skip and rescued by John Strover, trustee of the Mitcham Cricket Green Community and Heritage Society. The photos can now be viewed online at the Merton Memories photographic archive.

THE KING'S HEAD

18 Merton High Street, SW19 1DN

While the earliest records of this pub are from the start of the eighteenth century, there are claims that it was the oldest pub in Wimbledon, dating back to 1496. It has been suggested there may have been some sort of tavern here in that era which sold the excess ale produced by monks at the adjacent Merton Priory and that lineage was being claimed back to that establishment.

The pub was taken on by Young's in 1831 and rebuilt by them in 1934. Clive Whichelow's book *Pubs of Wimbledon Town* includes a reference to a regular here who told a local history project in the 1980s there used to be a large stage at the back of the pub where shows took place every Saturday. This included drivers from the bus garage next door who put on musical shows here and had their own theatre company!

Sadly the curtain came down on the King's Head in 2004. Both CAMRA and the Sutton Acoustic Music Group, who used the pub for events, protested, but Young's stated they didn't see a viable way to keep it open. It has since been converted into offices for the bus garage next door. There is no indication as to whether the drivers have made the most of this space to continue their predecessors' musical traditions.

KING OF DENMARK

83 Ridgway, SW19 4ST

Dating from 1866, the pub also served as the inspiration for the names of the nearby streets Denmark Terrace and Denmark Road.

It was rebuilt in the 1930s and it was in this incarnation where it welcomed the then King of Denmark in the 1960s alongside his daughter Princess Marguerite. This information is recorded in Clive Whichelow's other excellent book on pubs in this area, *Pubs of Wimbledon Village* – although he was unable to uncover the reason for the visit.

Whichelow goes on to mention that the pub had another high-profile Scandinavian visitor in 1972, namely that year's Miss Denmark! The landlord during this decade, Jack Fuller (a fine surname for a connection to a pub), was said to cook sausages and potatoes on an open fire for his customers, which sounds a very homely welcome.

Talking of high-profile visitors, the King was also once one of the 'Wimbledon Eight', a favoured pub crawl by the actor and legendary hellraiser Oliver Reed. It certainly would have been a lively night if he'd dropped in when either the royal or beauty queens were visiting.

In its final years it was described as retaining its traditional feel with wood panelling, darts and a lack of gimmicks. The pub closed in 2007. An initial application for demolition and replacement with flats was rejected by Merton Council but granted on appeal and the pub was levelled in 2011. There was originally due to be a restaurant on the ground floor of the block but the application was rejected and by the end of 2017 the space was occupied by a Co-op.

MARQUIS OF LORNE

117 Haydons Road, SW19 1HH

This opened in the late Victorian period as this part of Wimbledon continued to expand. In the 1970s it started offering a cockney flavour to this part of south west London, with a musician here on weeknight evenings belting out old East End favourites like *Knees Up Mother Brown*.

In an ironic twist given the final fate of the pub, Clive Whichelow wrote that it was popular with local policemen and the word on the beat got around to the extent that bobbies were even coming down from Scotland Yard to enjoy the atmosphere here.

The police were again visitors to the pub during the noughties but this time for all the wrong reasons due to it becoming a hotbed of violent activity and drug dealing, which led to the licence being revoked in 2007. An article in the *Wimbledon Guardian* from 2009 recalled an incident where the premise was stormed by 100 police officers in riot gear. Weapons such as machetes, an air rifle and even a crossbow were also found on the site. There was also underage drinking taking place, but if I were a Merton teenager, I think the local recreation ground would have been a safer bet.

The building then lay derelict for over a decade until permission was granted in late 2019 for construction of flats on the site while still retaining the front and side façade of the pub.

THE OUTRIGGER

30 Thames Side, KT1 1PX

First opened in 1864 on the Kingston riverbank, it was rebuilt in 1927 and served as a refreshment point for the scores of people working on that part of the river back then.

In a retrospective piece for *The News Shopper* local paper, June Sampson described her recollection of the place during the 1970s and '80s. She stated it was still very much a waterman's pub even though a lot of the wharfs had already closed by this stage. The interior was decorated with old ropes, charts, navigation lights and other items brought in by the regulars with their riparian connections.

During this period the landlord was a Mr Roy Stringer, also known as Captain Carruthers, who was in charge here for a quarter of a century. Accounts of Stringer from online sources describe him as a character who often welcomed famous visitors to the pub like Danny La Rue and Reg Varney.

The pub was also the meeting point for the annual activity of 'Swan Upping', which effectively acts as a census of cygnets on this stretch of the Thames. This tradition continues today and is carried out by representatives of the King as well as from the Vinters and Dyers, the two City of London livery companies which also have ownership rights over mute swans on the river.

During the 1970s the then Prince Charles even dropped in for the Upping. Captain C, being the consummate landlord, even served up the then Prince of Wales a portion of jellied eels. It is reported the future King was not particularly taken with this delicacy.

The Outrigger had closed by early 2000 and by the end of that year was purchased by the Bentalls Centre, the nearby huge shopping centre. They obtained permission to demolish it, at the time stating there were a number of possibilities for the site but in reality it has simply been subsumed into a car park.

THE ST HELIER ARMS

299 Middleton Road, SM5 1HW

The suburban fringes of south west London would seem an unlikely location for Britain's roughest pub but that was the claim made by *The Independent* newspaper in 1994. In these final days it was known as the St Helier Tavern.

It all started with such noble aims too. It first opened in 1937 to serve the new St Helier estate. The LCC had leased a plot of land of the estate to the 'Improved Public House Company', with the building also incorporating a tearoom, no doubt to encourage sober socialising for estate residents.

The article in *The Independent* outlined the decline of the pub over time. It was already attracting trouble by the 1970s to the extent the pub was boarded up for a year as the brewery couldn't find anyone to manage it. For a spell in the 1980s a nineteen stone Welshman called Alvin Williams managed to keep a relative lid on things. However after five years had had enough and left.

The brewery then put Carlo Spetali in charge but things only escalated further. In 1992 a man who'd previously worked with Mr Williams was shot at point blank range by one of the bouncers, and then the murderer and associates cut the body up in a suitably grizzly manner. Incredibly Spetali described two of the men involved as 'keepers of the peace' at the pub.

It had its licence revoked for the last time in Spring 1994 but not before two more men had been battered in an attack involving a stiletto knife and a pool cue.

It was demolished in 1996 and replaced by flats. The locals interviewed for *The Independent* weren't sad about the prospect of the pub going, with one saying the best thing to do would be levelling the pub and putting a police station there instead.

THE TOBY JUG

1 Hook Rise South, KT5 9PB

Never underestimate the ability of a suburban pub to surprise you. The Toby Jug in Tolworth opened in 1934 as Greater London's urban sprawl edged ever closer to Surrey. However it was far from sleepy suburbia here!

Firstly it was a key location in the Harry Houghton spy case, a British naval officer who was a spy for both Poland and the Soviet Union during the Cold War as part of the Portland spy ring. The Toby Jug was one of the places where Houghton passed on his information about Britain's nuclear submarine secrets to Soviet agents. Houghton was arrested in 1961 and three years later the whole affair was made into a film called *Ring of Spies* which duly featured The Toby Jug as part of the story.

Later in the decade it also became a prominent live music venue, something slightly more in keeping with other suburban pubs featured here. In a pivotal night in his career, David Bowie performed here on 10 February 1972 with the live debut of his Ziggy Stardust persona and kicked off a tour that lasted for the next eighteen months. Other major bands played here in their early days, including Led Zeppelin, although according to an article from the *Surrey Live* website in 2022 looking back at the pub's history, the band's name was misspelt as Led Zepplin!

The pub was unable to continue to scale such heights during the 1980s and '90s and closed down in 2001. The land was bought by Tesco for a supermarket, with the pub demolished the following year, but the supermarket never arrived and the site lay vacant.

In recent years it joined the select group of London pubs to have a book written about it. *Hello Tolworth, I'm Ziggy* by Tim Harrison was published in 2016 and recounts the history of the pub from birth to demolition, with all the juicy bits in between too.

THE WOODSTOCK

1 Stonecot Hill, SM3 9HB

It seems somewhat appropriate that given the name, this former pub's biggest claim to fame comes from a huge band performing here in the 1960s at the very start of their career.

It first opened in 1936, on the site of a manor house of the same name. The builders of the pub, the Brentford Brewery, reused the decorated tiles of the manor house for the ceiling of their 'Victoriana Lounge'. It was described by CAMRA as being a spacious pub in the 1930s roadhouse style.

By the 1960s it was playing host to regular live music, including the Rolling Stones on 5 October 1962, one of their earliest gigs, having only formed as a band earlier that year.

The Woodstock was still hosting live music events well into the noughties. In 2014 ASDA fixed their eyes on it as a perfect location for a new mini supermarket. A local campaign was launched to save the pub but was unsuccessful as Sutton Council granted planning permission to the supermarket giant's plans in January 2015 and the pub had been demolished by that summer.

BROMLEY AND CROYDON

THE FORUM

Trinity Square, Whitgift Centre, CR0 1LP

In the 1960s Croydon was at the heart of a building boom with office blocks and shopping centres popping up left, right and centre. One of them, the Whitgift Centre, even included its own pub, The Forum.

This blocky building, which some people labelled as a UFO, was located in the middle of the open-air shopping centre. It was a multi-level pub which featured the novelty of getting there via a travelator from the lowest level of the centre. It was given a loosely Roman theme, hence the name Forum.

Online accounts vary as to the extent of its opening hours. Some articles state the pub was tied in with those of the Whitgift so it closed when the shops shut at 6pm. However other stories have people reminiscing about the pub being open on Friday night for a disco.

At the start of the 1990s it was renamed The Merchant but it only had three years in this guise before closing. The trends in the shopping centre world were changing and open air was out and indoor was, well, in. This saw the construction of an atrium at the heart of the centre with The Forum cleared away to put it in.

THE GOAT HOUSE

2 Penge Road, SE25 4BQ

This first opened in 1864 and was described as an impressive imposing three storey building located close to the railway line. There had previously been a Goat House Farm (which itself had its own licenced premise) located close by to the pub.

The pub was rebuilt in 1936 and for many years it managed to live up to its name by having a couple of goats in the pub's garden. These went in the mid-1990s when it was turned into a car park. The Goat House was hit by misfortune when it was damaged by a large fire while being refurbished in July 1996.

The pub was restored and was back up and running again by the end of the year. It also featured in a few *Time Out* guides in the early noughties, an impressive achievement given the scarcity of pubs in the outer fringes that make it into these kind of books. The reviews tended to focus on it being a large, open plan establishment featuring table football and multiple pool tables as well as the hearty, traditional pub grub on offer.

The pub closed for good in 2004 and was demolished three years later with a block of flats built in its place. The Goat House heritage has been remembered in the shape of the Shelverdine Goathouse, a pub which opened nearby in 2016 on the site of a former Wetherspoons.

THE GUN

83 Church Street, CR0 1RN

First popped up on the scene in the 1880s, The Gun came into its own from the 1970s and '80s onwards as a notable venue for live music.

On a Croydon history Facebook group, members recalled seeing huge names like David Bowie during his early days, a fact which is verified by a website dedicated to the artist called 'The Bowie Bible' which dated this as 18 November 1969. A *MyLondon* retrospective piece on the pub published online in August 2022

recalled someone popping into the pub once, only to see Rick Parfitt from Status Quo having a drink!

This same article also featured a collection of memories of the pub's less appealing side, with online reviews from the noughties bemoaning the poor state of the beer or calling it a tired, depressing place. A more positive view was provided by an assistant manager of the pub in the early 2000s who said that on Sundays the pub served up live music in the shape of big band jazz, alongside a traditional roast dinner.

Time was called on The Gun by the early 2010s and the building has been used as a variety of different restaurants. Its present guise is a Romanian restaurant called Mahala.

THE PROPELLER

449 Purley Way, CR0 4RG

The name here was very fitting as the pub had close links to Croydon's aviation past. It first opened in 1936, located next to the local airport and soon became popular with RAF personnel based there during the Second World War.

The airport closed back in 1959 but the pub continued trading for many years after. An online testimony written by a former licensee of the pub stated there was an extensive refurbishment of the pub in 1982, with interior features restored and even a De Havilland propeller displayed above the mantelpiece.

The Propeller suffered from an arson attack in 2001 which proved to be the death knell for the pub as it never reopened. After it lay derelict for five years plans were brought forward for its replacement with housing. These plans brought dismay from users of the UK website Key Aero, an aviation news website, with enthusiasts wanting the pub preserved for its links to the RAF and the Aerodrome.

These efforts were not successful and the pub was demolished in 2007. A leisure centre now stands on the site. These days the only wings you'll see round here are Wing-Yip, the huge Chinese supermarket based on Purley Way.

THE SAXON TAVERN

Southend Lane, SE6 2DD

A true hothouse of entertainment in this corner of south London, the Saxon hosted not only live music but comedians as well as DJ nights too. It began life as The King Alfred, opening just after the Second World War. It was renamed The Saxon Tavern by the 1970s. It managed to draw in some major comedians of the day, including Les Dawson, Bob Monkhouse and Larry Grayson.

On the music side, a suitably wide range of genres aired here from jazz, soul, ska, as well as a bit of out and out rock. It is remembered fondly across London with posts across multiple online forums remembering 'Del Stevens' rock roadshow'. In 1985 it hosted a seminal show for a legendary south London band as Squeeze performed their reunion gig here on 12 January.

The pub closed by the mid-1990s, lying derelict for several years before a fire destroyed the building. The Saxon's spot is now occupied by a Lidl.

SWAN & SUGAR LOAF

Brighton Road, CR2 6EA

An impressive late Victorian building, the Swan & Sugar Loaf held court over this area for over 100 years. It was built by Overton's, a brewery located in the heart of Croydon on Surrey Street.

It replaced an earlier pub of the same name which accounts suggest was far less interesting from an architectural perspective. Geoff Brandwood and Jane Jephcote described the pub in *London's Heritage Pubs* as 'dramatically designed' for its fork in the road location. The entry heaped particular praise on the snug area with its Jacobean style fireplace and six seats which they felt were like the 'drinkers'

version of a chapter house in an Abbey', as well as mentioning the stained glass window depicting two swans and a loaf of sugar.

Shortly after the book was published the pub shut in March 2010 as its owners went into administration. The building was then squatted in for a period in 2011 until the occupants were evicted in the wake of the riots that August. Scaffolding went up later that year to restore the building after its recent wear and tear, and a quote given to the *Inside Croydon* website said it hadn't been decided whether it would reopen as a pub or a restaurant.

In the end it was neither as it was reborn as a Tesco Express in 2012. The Swan & Sugar Loaf name still lives on, both at the top of the building as well as being the name of a TfL bus stop.

THE THREE TUNS

157 High Street, BR3 1AE

While David Bowie was born in Brixton, it was in another south London 'B', Beckenham, where he performed on numerous occasions at this very pub in the early part of his career. The Three Tuns first opened in the early 1830s before being rebuilt in the interwar period with the mock Tudor frontage which was so popular with breweries at that time that it was nicknamed 'Brewers Tudor'.

It was at the end of the 1960s when Bowie started appearing here most Sundays as part of what was originally called The Folk Club before being rechristened the Beckenham Arts Lab. Bowie appeared here up until 1973. There was other musical entertainment here during the sixties with an entry on the Lost Pubs website recalling excellent jazz nights which took place here.

During the 1990s the pub was renamed the Rat and Parrot, a chain of pubs which had several branches across Greater London and beyond. A plaque marking Bowie's connection was put up outside the pub in December 2001. It had a brief stint back with its original name before closing for good in 2003. The next year it became a branch of Zizzi's restaurant, which saw the plaque taken down before eventually being put up again in 2010. After Bowie's death in January 2016, the pavement outside the pub was filled with floral tributes.

OUTER SOUTH EAST (BEXLEY, GREENWICH, LEWISHAM)

THE BARGE POLE

32 Corraline Walk, SE2 9SU

As an area, Thamesmead quickly acquired a poor reputation, with a combination of bad transport links, the growing unease at big brutalist estates from the late 1960s onwards and its use as a filming location for *A Clockwork Orange* in 1973 all conspiring against it.

As a flat roof pub at the end of one of the estates, it is easy to pigeonhole the Barge Pole in with the perception of these kind of pubs, best summed up in the magazine *Viz*. Memories on local Abbey Wood Facebook pages were divided about the pub, a fair few people sticking up for the place or saying it was a great pub in the 1970s whereas others recounted less appealing incidents there such as walking in on an organised dog fight or suggesting you needed to wipe your feet on the way out. Another poster recalled seeing Jim Davidson performing there in the early days of his career – I'll leave it to you to decide whether that's a tick or a cross against the Barge Pole.

It was reviewed in 2013 by PubSpy, a feature that did the rounds across various local newspapers owned by Newsquest and which at times could come across fairly sneering in tone. The anonymous hack's verdict here was bordering on positive although it was a slightly contradictory piece. In one passage they referred to the interior being 'clean' with a 'pleasing nautical theme' yet in the next sentence noting it as 'dingy' with 'miserable' carpets and a 'lingering smell of urine'.

A year later it made it onto the silver screen as a location in a David Essex film called *The Guvnors*, a film about football hooliganism and gang rivalry. In January 2018 the Barge Pole closed and was demolished by the summer of that year. It was swallowed up as part of the wider Peabody plans which also involved the demolition of the housing blocks beside it which are going to be replaced with new housing.

THE DIRECTOR GENERAL

55 Wellington Street, SE18 6PQ

Not named after the top dog at the BBC, rather the name given to an impressive gun that previously stood within the Royal Arsenal and dated from the late Victorian era. It had an ornate interior and was popular with staff at the printing press located across the road. In its later years it also became known as a gay friendly venue.

The DG found itself in the line of fire when it was announced in 2007 it would be demolished as part of a major redevelopment of Woolwich Town centre. The local MP and other members of the community spoke out against the loss of a traditional London pub with so many original features still intact. There were also calls for some of the heritage features such as the stained-glass windows to be preserved in the replacement pub planned as part of the redevelopment.

Regrettably these items were not saved and the pub was demolished in 2008. The Tesco superstore built on this site subsequently went on to win the Carbuncle Cup for the ugliest new building of 2014, so there you go.

THE MONTAGUE ARMS

289 Queen's Road, SE15 2PA

In 2008 this New Cross institution found itself No.1 in *The Rough Pub Guide*, a book written by Paul Moody and Robin Turner. As mentioned when the book was referenced earlier, this was meant more as a term of endearment than a slight.

The pub first opened in the 1860s and it was around a hundred years later when it passed into the hands of Peter Hoyle, who turned it into a thriving live music venue and away from being full of gangsters.

They had comedians here too including Mike Reid and Jim Davidson, who certainly got around several of the pubs featured in this book. The NME used the pub in 1989 for a roundtable interview between Nick Cave, Mark E. Smith and Shane McGowan, further cementing its legitimacy as a cult venue.

The *Rough Pub Guide* marvelled at the eccentric interior décor, from a real human skeleton perched on the bar through to an embalmed zebra peering out from a horse drawn carriage, plenty more taxidermy and an old deep sea diver outfit.

Right up until and through the noughties Peter played here alongside his friend Peter London in a band called The Two Petes. Moody and Turner describe how on New Year's Eve 2007 they played an eclectic mix of songs from *The Lambeth Walk* (oi!) to *Wonderwall.*

All was well here until 2018 when it was revamped as a gastropub and the cluttered, quirky interior swept away and given a new minimalist vibe and with live music off the agenda. Regrettably I never made it here but I remember similar refurb jobs at places like The Three Kings in Clerkenwell and Sir Richard Steele in Belsize Park and how much of the character and spirit of the place can be lost in the process.

The new look Montague Arms didn't fare too well and closed by the summer of 2019. Since then plans have been brought forward for demolition of the pub and its replacement with flats and a smaller new pub. This generated a huge backlash in the local community and the plans were withdrawn in April 2021.

A revised plan which would have seen the existing pub refurbished but with the upper floors converted into flats was also withdrawn in 2022 and the pub lies derelict but intact. Could this quirky place rise again in a new incarnation? I'll be keeping my fingers crossed.

RAILWAY TAVERN

Forest Road, DA8 2NU

When the Railway first came to Slade Green at the start of the twentieth century, the industrious South Eastern Railway Company also built 300 houses for rail workers as well as this pub hotel.

Within a few years of opening, the landlord found himself in trouble with the law. As James Packer outlined in his book *Lost Pubs of Bexley*, the publican was fined £1 for selling under-proof whiskey, although it was proved to be due to his poor eyesight, meaning he couldn't read the true figures for breaking down the whiskey. These days I think eyebrows might be raised at that line of defence!

A photo of the pub's sign from the 1980s has been uploaded to the *Dover Kent Archives* website, with an InterCity 125 train being illustrated on the sign. A fine train this was for sure, but the self-proclaimed 'Journey Shrinker' never travelled on the North Kent Lines.

In a response to a post about the pub from the Bexley Archives on Facebook, Mark Selby recalled popping in there after work one day in 1998 shortly after buying a house nearby and in his own words 'I have never been made to feel so unwelcome in a pub', going on to add it felt like he'd walked into a 'Western Saloon'.

The pub closed early in the new millennium. There was an initial application to convert the pub into a ten-bedsit hostel in 2001 which was rejected by Bexley Council. A later application for conversion into apartments was successful and this work took place in 2006.

THE ROYAL GEORGE

2 Blissett Street, SE10 8UP

Dating from the early nineteenth century, this pub was a long-time staple of the Greenwich pub scene.

When it popped up in the *Fancyapint?* guide of 2006, it was referred to as an excellent little local with the attractive stained-glass windows and model ships

giving its interior character. Online reviews covering the same period also were in broad agreement about the place being a hidden gem and a welcoming spot just off from the main Greenwich tourist trail.

The pub closed just weeks into the 2010s. The owners Shepherd Neame then applied for planning permission to convert the building into flats. As part of their evidence that the pub had become unviable, they cited figures that the pub had gone through on average 120 beer barrels a year during the noughties. By comparison in the period between 1977 and 1986, it had been reaching up to 310 barrels.

Approval was granted by Greenwich Council in March 2010. Following the conversion the Royal George signage has still been retained at the very top of the building, as well as the Shepherd Neame logo.

THE WAT TYLER

21 Telemann Square, SE3 8YR

Built as a new pub as part of the Ferrier Estate in Kidbrooke that was completed in 1972, it was named after the leader of the peasants' revolt who had assembled his men at nearby Blackheath.

Local accounts suggest the pub started off on a decent footing as a community hub for the local area. However it was seen to go downhill from the mid-1980s in line with the growing issues that were facing the estate itself. From my research it showed up across several 'roughest pubs' posts across multiple different south London football clubs online forums.

It closed in 2000 and stood derelict until finally being demolished in 2013 as the wrecking ball moved into the entire Ferrier Estate. During its derelict years it was used as a backdrop in *The Firm,* one of the many noughties' films about football hooligans.

THE WHITE HART HOTEL

184 New Cross Road, SE14 5AA

Thought to be New Cross's oldest pub, the White Hart occupied a prime position on the junction between New Cross Road and Queens Road. When the current building first opened in the 1860s, it was located next to the Toll Gate that gave New Cross Gate its name.

The pub was Grade II listed in the 1990s, which referenced the building's 'elaborate parapet'. CAMRA also rated the pub as having an interior of special national historic interest, noting cast iron gold columns in the servery area as well as the back bar remaining largely intact with very old mirrors.

The pub had a very brief and ill-fated conversion into a strip club during the early months of 2009, the owners having successfully appealed the original decision to reject the proposal. It was back to being a pub by the summer of 2009 and local blogger Transpont speculated that it may have been the building's listed status that hampered these plans, as blacked-out windows would not have been allowed.

In the mid-2010s it was refreshed and, under the stewardship of Patrick and Joseph Ryan, was focused on providing an extensive range of keg beers, some of which were brewed on site. The pub also had a wide variety of live music including Irish folk music and jazz nights, as well as DJs playing here on Friday and Saturday nights until 3am.

When the owners of the pub, the Wellington Pub Company, announced plans in 2019 to turn the upper floors of the building into flats, people were naturally concerned about the long-term prospects for the pub with the potential for noise complaints and more restrictive licence conditions stifling the place. Over 3,000 people signed a petition against the plans and Lewisham Council rejected them that August. The pub's website is still accessible online which includes an image of someone holding a white can of beer with the text #SAVETHEHART written on it.

Sadly the story didn't end there and the owners appealed against the original decision, with the planning inspector finding in their favour and overruling Lewisham's ruling, while recognising that the flats would mean that only acoustic music would be allowed here and not after 11pm. The inspector thought this would still allow a pub to be viable here but the Ryans disagreed and closed up in December 2020.

WOOLWICH INFANT

9 Plumstead Road, SE18 7BZ

A name which doesn't have the meaning you'd first expect, it referred to a huge gun that was once *in situ* at the Woolwich Dockyard. Records suggest the pub opened in the early twentieth century. It was well placed right beside Woolwich's enduringly popular covered market. Towards the end of its life it became known as a gay friendly venue.

It featured in the first edition of *Derelict London* where Paul Talling said the first time he visited it he thought it was shut, only to find it was still open. He then visited a few years later where it looked in better health but the fact it featured in his book shows the revival didn't last long.

After closure it was converted into a clothes shop before becoming a branch of Sam's Chicken. For many years afterwards the Woolwich Infant sign still hung outside the chicken shop until it vanished in 2019.

THE WOODMAN

35 The Slade, SE18 2NB

One of the five 'Idlers' of Plumstead Common, where each of the pub names was concluded by a humorous suffix, this being The Woodman who never felled a tree. It was alongside The Star that never shone, The Ship that never sailed the sea, The Mill that never grinds the corn and then finally topped off with the Who'd a Thought it? as the end of the parable.

Records date the pub back to the 1850s. It existed happily enough with its four colleagues on the Common until well into the twenty-first century. It didn't seem to attract publicity, negative or positive, during its stint. The only thing of note I found was the fact it was where the Plumstead running club formed in 1987.

The pub closed in 2010 and was subsequently converted into an Indian restaurant. Signage remains visible at the top of the pub for The Woodman, lurking behind the vibrant red exterior.

NORTH EAST (HACKNEY, HARINGEY, WALTHAM FOREST)

THE ACORN

149 Queensbridge Road, E2 8PB

Dating from the early Victorian period, by all accounts this was a well-established locals pub. That said, online reviews of The Acorn were few and far between, with the only two on the prominent beerintheevening site coming from someone merely judging it from the exterior and another saying they hadn't visited for over twenty years.

The pub closed in early 2016 and by October that year an application had already gone in for it to be demolished and replaced by flats. CAMRA quickly jumped into action and got it listed as an ACV by Hackney Council two months later. At the time James Watson from the local CAMRA branch explained to a local newspaper that this was the first time in the country that ACV listing had saved a pub from demolition.

However the developers appealed the rejection of their plans and the planning inspector appointed by the Government agreed, saying the various alterations to the pub and its present cluttered appearance had undermined the historic relevance of the building and justified its demolition. Both CAMRA and the Hackney Society strongly criticised this finding, arguing that far too much was being made of these minor alterations which could be easily remedied.

The protests were in vain and the pub was demolished by February 2021.

THE ALEXANDRA

98 Fortis Green, N2 9EY

In the 1960s Muswell Hill was home to Ray and Dave Davies who formed the seminal English rock band The Kinks, and The Alexandra played a key role in the development of the band. The brothers used to come here for family gatherings where they'd all sing around the piano, something Dave later said had a lot of influence on the group. The pub first opened in 1864 with building work taking place during the 1920s following a road widening project.

The death knell came for the pub in 2014 when a company called STO Capital, based in the Cayman Islands, bought it and promptly put in an application to turn in into flats. Over 1,000 people signed a petition against the plans and Dave Davies spoke out, saying 'It would be tragic to lose this London asset'.

Haringey Council agreed and turned down the application. STO appealed and the Government inspector found in their favour, so the good times were gone for the pub as the conversion went ahead.

THE COCK TAVERN

67 High Street, E17 7DB

Starting life as a coaching inn during the mid-eighteenth century, the building that stands here today dates from the late Victorian era.

In the early 2000s the landlord at the time, Michael Adams, wanted to turn the upper floors of the pub into flats to help keep his head above water financially. This application was turned down by Waltham Forest Council on account of the pub being in a conservation area. He then received funding from the EU to refurbish the building to the tune of £120,000, with Adams contributing £20,000 of his own money.

In 2016 the owner of the pub announced to Adams' successor that it would be closing in three months' time. It closed in August that year, with many expressing their dismay in the local media, saying it was taking away a meeting point for the community and in particular older people who'd been going there for decades. One woman recounted an Irish gent who'd been going there for thirty years and had started crying at the prospect of losing his local.

It was then quickly approved for conversion to retail use. Mr Adams felt it was hypocritical that it was so easy for that to happen, when his plan for flats which would have kept the pub trading were blocked. For their part the Council explained that as the pub wasn't an ACV, there was nothing to prevent a change of use for the building. It's now a cake shop, with the model of a cockerel still at the upper part of the building, a reminder of its past life.

THE COLEGRAVE ARMS

145 Cann Hall Road, E11 3NJ

This Leytonstone local served the community for over 100 years. CAMRA characterised it as a Victorian pub which had been given a rather plain refit in the 1930s. That said, they were more impressed by the preserved mirrors advertising Charrington's beers, as well as the fact it was still divided into three separate rooms with their thirties fittings all still intact.

When it closed in 2010, a war of words started with the new owners of the building, the Cann Hall Deen and Educational Trust, who claimed it had been a hotbed of antisocial behaviour which led to its closure. Its last landlady, Julie Edmondson, told the local paper that the pub shut down solely because the pubco owner Enterprise was looking to cut costs by selling off some of their pubs. She insisted there had never been any trouble there and one of the former regulars interviewed for the same article agreed and called it a 'proper community pub'.

The Trust succeeded in their aspiration to convert the building into a mosque, which opened just over a year after last orders had been called at The Colegrave.

THE DEURAGON ARMS

9 Shepherds Lane, E9 6JJ

This interwar Homerton pub really broke into its stride from the 1950s onwards when it became a regular haunt for live music and cabaret-style entertainment as well as drag acts including Gay Travers.

In 1968 Martin Green and Tony White described the variety of entertainment that had been on offer in the pub during that decade from bands like the marvellously named Bonzo Dog Doo Dah Band through to go-go dancers in gilded cages. The Lost Pubs Project has various stories from people who recall seeing live acts here, one even stating they saw Keith Moon from the Who visit once and that Moon then went on to destroy the drums of the band who were playing that night.

The pub closed in the mid-1990s and was demolished in 2015 to make way for a pocket home development, an initiative being trialled at several locations in London aimed at creating more affordable flats, albeit at a smaller size.

THE FISHMONGERS ARMS

287 High Road, N22 8HU

Taking its name from nearby almshouses built by the Fishmongers livery company, the pub first opened in 1855.

In the 1920s a dance hall was built at the back of the pub called Bourne Hall which by the 1940s was home to the Wood Green jazz club. The following decade the pub's upstairs rooms were used by jazz musicians, including the legendary Humphrey Lyttleton. The pub and its jazz scene featured in a short 25-minute film funded by the BFI called *Momma Don't Allow.*

In the 1960s rock became the name of the game with early performances with bands starting out on their way to stardom, including Fleetwood Mac, the Kinks, Led Zeppelin and Pink Floyd.

The venue went through some alternative names in the subsequent decades including the Barracuda and Fagans. In its final days it was called O'Raffertys, an Irish pub.

It closed for good in the mid-noughties. The upper floors were converted to flats with the ground floor becoming a police station, certainly the only pub to police station conversion in this book!

THE FOX

372 Kingsland Road, E8 4DA

The current building dates from 1881 but the story goes that there has been a Fox pub in one guise or another on Kingsland Road for hundreds of years.

The landlord from the 1960s to the early 1980s, Clifford Saxe, was implicated in some very high-profile crimes, including the Security Express robbery in 1983. Shortly after this he decided to retire to Spain while he still had his freedom. The next year the police broke through a false wall in the pub and discovered a secret compartment where they thought the loot had been hidden. This room smelt of old beer and mildew and during the trial of the gang suspected of the robbery, the police claimed that some of the banknotes they'd recovered had that same aroma, suggesting they'd been stored in the Fox.

As the local area changed, the pub gradually got more upmarket and in 2012 it was relaunched as a craft beer hotspot. An online *Time Out* review from 2015 called it a 'very worthy pub' and 'much beloved locally', with a neat little roof terrace.

All was going well until June 2018 when it was suddenly announced the pub had to close for at least a year to allow for the upstairs to be converted into flats by the owners of the building and the necessary structural renovations to allow this. The statement by the pub's management on social media said they'd done everything they could to fight it but assured their regulars the pub would be back.

Given you're reading about it here, the pub has clearly not returned but at the very least the ground floor hasn't been converted into flats too, so The Fox is down but not definitely out.

THE HAPPY MAN

89 Woodberry Grove, N4 2SB

Built in 1957 as part of the Woodberry Down estate, it also had a spell known as the Blarney Stone and Bechers.

The pub's Facebook account from the 2010s is still online and paints a picture of a lively pub showing football and horse racing as well as DJ nights, karaoke and even the occasional drag queen. The photos also show off the small but perfectly formed beer garden.

Hackney Council first agreed plans for the wholesale demolition of the Woodberry Down estate in 2009; given the scale of the site, this was broken down into several phases. The bell tolled for the Happy Man in 2019 when plans were approved for its demolition as part of this phase of the development. It closed that July and had been demolished by September 2020.

The Happy Man name has lived on in a slightly unexpected epilogue. The redevelopment plans for the area also included removal of a tree outside the pub. It was estimated to be over 150 years old so significantly older than the pub itself. A community group came together to try to save the Happy Man tree. It was even named the Woodland Trust's Tree of the Year for 2020. This was not enough to stop

the tree being felled the following year but the community group who attempted to save it have kept its legacy alive by making a short film about the last months of the tree, which they released in October 2023.

THE HORNSEY WOOD TAVERN

376 Seven Sisters Road, N4 2PQ

This pub had its initial roots back in 1750 as a tavern within the Hornsey Wood. The tavern was rebuilt at the end of that century as a larger building which formed part of what was now a private leisure park complete with a fishing and boating lake. That in turn was felled in 1866 to make the whole area part of the new Finsbury Park.

A new pub was soon built on the Seven Sisters Road opposite the park and stood here for over 130 years. In the 1960s it was another pub that boasted a great live music scene, with artists and bands like Jeff Beck, Jethro Tull and Led Zeppelin playing here during that decade.

In its later years it was known as the Alexandra Bar and picked up some positive online reviews for its Thai food, as well as references to live music still featuring here. The pub closed in 2007 and was demolished soon after to be replaced by a block of flats.

LORD BROOKE

47 Shernhall Street, E17 3EY

This Walthamstow pub opened in the late nineteenth century. It was briefly called the Greyhound and Hare before being renamed during the 1880s as the then Lord Brooke (Francis Greville) married Frances Maynard in 1881 who just happened to be heiress to 560 acres of land in the manor of Walthamstow.

It featured in Peter Haydon's 1996 London Pub Guide where he said the place 'exudes a warm welcome' as well as noting the games room full of trophies won by the pub's darts team. CAMRA's summary was similar, labelling it a 'large, well-appointed Victorian local'.

Warm welcomes may have been slightly thinner on the ground in the pub's final days. The licence was revoked in Spring 2014 after the police labelled it 'a drug haven' after carrying out a raid where they found it littered with drug paraphernalia with dealers living upstairs too. Talking of the upper floors, this was another area the owners fell foul of the law. After they acquired the pub in 2010, they tried to get planning permission for its conversion into a hostel. This was refused. Despite this the owners still set up a £15 a night hostel above the pub, the existence of which was confirmed during the same raid.

Initial plans to convert it into a Buddhist temple were blocked by Waltham Forest's planning committee. The building finally returned into use in October 2022 as the Lotusbloom Cafe.

THE PRINCE EDWARD

97 Wick Road, E9 5AB

This Victorian pub was labelled Hackney's last 'working class pub' when it celebrated its 150th birthday in 2016.

By this point it had established itself as a popular haunt for the area's Afro-Caribbean community. As James Watson from the local CAMRA branch told me, it was the sort of place where you'd find older gents playing dominoes till 2am while reggae music played. The Hackney Irish Social Club also met here.

The first storm clouds on the horizon for the Prince emerged two years before the birthday celebrations. The owner unveiled plans to demolish the pub and replace it with a block of flats with two cafés on the ground floor. Following a concerted effort by the local community, it was listed as an ACV in 2015.

The pub closed in 2018 with the owner bringing forward an alternative proposal that would retain the pub but build additional stories on top of it as well as a new block in the garden. Planning permission was granted for these changes with the work largely completed by the autumn of 2023. A pub could yet reopen here but in James' view it will have inevitably lost the community spirit that existed here before.

THE SHIP

499 High Road, N17 6QA

This former Tottenham pub can claim an impressive historical lineage. The first instance of a pub with this name on the High Road was way back in 1610, when it served as a coaching inn on the route between London and Cambridge.

The present building dates from the late Victorian period and its architectural merit has put it on CAMRA's pub inventory list. It has an impressive green tiled exterior while elements of the interior noted by CAMRA include an old Taylor Walker mirror and the curved island bar in the centre with its wooden countertop.

Online reviews of the pub over the last decade or so noted it was a bit tatty and rough around the edges but with great potential if someone had some money to give it a bit of tlc. It was said to be very busy when Spurs were playing at home but much quieter aside from those peak periods.

More recently it looks like they were branching out to having live music here with various performances listed on their Facebook page from 2022 with a selection of artists playing mainly acoustic sets in the pub's garden. They were also cashing in on gigs taking place at Spurs' new stadium with posts of people popping in after mega shows like Guns N' Roses and Lady Gaga.

The pub closed abruptly in February 2023. There has been little communication since so hopefully this Ship could sail again in the near future.

SHIP AGROUND

144 Lea Bridge Road, E5 9RB

First opened in 1871, the pub occupied a prime spot to serve the industries that once existed around this part of Clapton as well as being a stone's throw away from the River Lea.

It was reportedly a favourite of the ska singer Buster Bloodvessel and his band Bad Manners during the 1980s. This was another pub James Watson mentioned to me and he remembered it as an old school place which made toasted sandwiches and was popular with the local workers, a bit down at heel but with a solid atmosphere. By the noughties it had acquired a Caribbean theme with jerk chicken and pork served up and had a decent reputation based on several online reviews.

The pub closed in late 2009 and permission was given for its conversion into a Sikh temple. Work began but then ground to a halt after the roof of the pub had been taken off as the owners reportedly ran out of cash.

Over a decade on, the building remains in this state of limbo. The shell of the pub remains, covered in scaffolding and still minus a roof. There have been various statements issued over the course of the last decade that the conversion is still going to happen but no further progress has been made. For now it stands a bit like a pub version of Battersea Power Station before the restoration, minus its roof and exposed to the elements.

THE VICTORIA

28 North Hill, N6 4QA

This cosy former Highgate pub dates to the mid-point of the nineteenth century and it was rebuilt in its current form in the early twentieth century.

Its review in the 1987 Nicholson guide called it rather upmarket and offering 'numerous delights' including six real ales and a beer garden at the back. Michael Harrison, Vice President of Highgate Society, told me it was very popular during the 1990s and did good pub food.

In 2013 the new manager at the time Barry Gill turned the pub into a popular live music venue. The *Ham and High* reported that a Kinks night held here even saw Ray Davies himself popping in. The pub shut abruptly in January 2017, where Mr Gill found himself locked out of his own establishment. Planning permission was granted the next year for a rear extension of the pub to be demolished to allow the building of flats behind and above the pub.

The Highgate Society and other local campaigners attempted to get it listed as an ACV after its closure in 2017 with over 100 people signing a petition. This was unsuccessful as was a subsequent attempt four years later. Presently the pub lies derelict with minimal signs of activity regarding the construction of flats at the back.

OUTER EAST
(BARKING AND DAGENHAM/ HAVERING/ NEWHAM/ REDBRIDGE)

THE BRITANNIA

1 Church Street, IG11 8PR

For many years this was the most easterly London outpost of Young's, a brewery synonymous with south west London.

It first opened in the middle of the nineteenth century before being rebuilt at the end of the 1890s and acquiring its most distinctive architectural feature. The architect was Frederick W. Ashton and he included a set of caryatids (a sculptured female figure to anyone like me who didn't study classics) flanking the pub's exterior. Ashton included this feature in several of his other pub/hotel buildings including the Duke of Fife in Upton Park, which is now a Paddy Power with a budget hotel above it. These caryatids are topless, which led to the pub's local nickname to reportedly be 'Tits' according to Young's historian Helen Osborn.

Speaking of Young's, they acquired the pub in 1965 and promptly put an advert in the local paper asking for anyone with historical information about the pub to get in touch, with a £5 promised as a reward. The advert closed by saying this was for genuine information only. Young's were obviously not taking any chances with people making up tall tales in exchange for a fiver, a decent sum in those days.

The pub frequently scooped up CAMRA Pub of the Year awards for east London during the noughties, and online reviews during this period were largely complimentary about a well-run, welcoming east London pub. The Britannia closed in October 2009. The building's exterior has been retained and it has now been incorporated into a neighbouring hotel which has expanded into the premises.

CAULIFLOWER

553 High Road, IG1 1TZ

Built on the site of a market and cauliflower patch, the present pub building here dates from 1900, replacing its predecessor from the previous century.

It first opened as a pub and hotel and was apparently a high-class establishment. This isn't hard to imagine given its impressive architectural presence. By the 1970s it had become a hotspot for live music; bands that played here included Ian Dury and the Blockheads, a local venue for Mr Dury who hailed from nearby Upminster.

When featured in *London's Heritage Pubs* in 2008, Geoff Brandwood and Jane Jephcote remarked it retained vestiges of a truly wonderful interior, including etched and polished glass alongside an impressive central bar. However they also pointed out that a few traditional looking features like the drinking alcoves had actually been put in during the latter half of the twentieth century.

The pub closed briefly in 2013 which led to locals fearing the worst, that it might become a Tesco Metro or McDonald's but it quickly reopened the following year with the youthful 18-year-old landlord called Reiss Matto pledging to restore it to its former glory. Disaster struck in 2018 when The Cauliflower was hit by a fire during the summer. Mr Matto was still the landlord but offered reassurance in the local media the damage had not been extensive and he hoped to reopen the pub by the end of the year.

This never happened and the pub remains shuttered. It is presently listed as available as a vacant pub via a property website. Thankfully at present there has been no talk of residential or retail conversion so this could flower again

THE DOCTOR JOHNSON

175 Longwood Gardens, IG5 0ES

Dating from 1938, The Doctor Johnson remained a well-preserved example of a pub from this era right up until its closure. It retained four separate rooms, the snug, the public bar, the saloon and the lounge, all with their own bar counter.

The name came from the fact one of the directors of Courage, the brewery that built the pub, was a fan of the author of the first dictionary. There are portraits of the great man himself in bas reliefs on the exterior of the pub. The Doctor Johnson was Grade II listed relatively late into its life in 2003. Interestingly the listing also included the pub's sign as well as the building itself.

The most glowing review I found of Doctor Johnson came from a website called Hairy Bar Snacks, where the authors are particularly keen on pubs which can supply such delights as pork scratchings and pickled eggs. The fact they still gave the good Doctor 10/10 despite him offering neither nibble shows how bowled over they were by the place. Picked out for particular praise were 'lovely revolving doors reminiscent of a posh hotel' as well as original Art Deco typography on the toilet doors.

The Doctor Johnson closed down in 2010, lying derelict for four years before squatters briefly entered with the aim of turning the building into a community centre. This didn't get very far and in 2019 part of the building reopened as a Co-op. The online listing on CAMRA's pub inventory site states that historic fittings in two rooms remain but they are now hidden behind the main use as a supermarket.

EARL OF ESSEX

616 Romford Road, E12 5AF

Built at the very start of the twentieth century, the Earl of Essex was rightly described by CAMRA as 'imposing' and a 'lavish architectural display'.

The organisation drew particular attention to the pub's corner turret and first floor balconies. The interior was also suitably impressive with ornate fireplaces, a decorative ceiling and a mosaic floored entrance. The building is also Grade II listed by Historic England, which was awarded in 1984.

The same entry from CAMRA's *London Heritage Pubs* acknowledged the pub was in a dilapidated state by the late noughties. Online reviews from the same period are mixed at best, a few people saying it was rough around the edges but that's what you want from an east London pub, but many were very critical of the quality of the beer.

The pub closed its doors in 2012 and was acquired by a company wanting to turn the upstairs into flats while reopening a pub on the ground floor. An initial application to do this was rejected by Newham Council in April 2018. Five months later the Earl found itself in the *Daily Mail* on account of the behaviour of squatters with neighbours thinking they must be holding sex parties there on account of the noises coming from the derelict pub. While this was mere speculation, it was confirmed they were trying to flog off the radiators and other old fittings from the pub on Gumtree, and the police stepped in to explain that would be selling stolen property. The listings swiftly vanished off Gumtree.

A revised application was approved by the council at the end of the year. The developers stated they'd got a company lined up to run the reopened pub, Brewit Microbrewery Ltd. Several years on and there is still no sign of a revived Earl of Essex.

MANBY ARMS

19 Water Lane, E15 4NL

This east London boozer opened in the early 1860s and, bar a short period during the Second World War, remained a fixture of the local pub scene for over 150 years.

In 1962 the pub had a pet donkey named Bass (after the incredibly popular ale of the time), which lived in the back yard but was occasionally beckoned in to perform his party trick, namely drinking beer from a glass. There is photographic proof of this online but sadly it is not clear from the picture whether the beer was Bass. As long as it wasn't Watney Red Barrel!

The pub had a mixed set of online reviews, from some saying it was a friendly place which put on sandwiches when West Ham were playing at home to those reporting it was plagued with drug dealers.

It was sold in 2013 for £1.25 million. The sales prospectus issued at the time kept the door alive to it staying as a pub, noting it still had a licence, but at the same time noting its potential for residential conversion and its proximity to Maryland Station, a future Crossrail Station.

Permission has been granted for its conversion into housing, retaining the pub's façade, but this work had still not begun at the time of writing.

THE OLD SPOTTED DOG

212 Upton Lane, E7 9NP

One of London's oldest pubs, dating back to the sixteenth century and steeped in history.

The pub was first established when this part of town was very much countryside (the Eastenders map would have looked very different). It is said the tavern was first opened here by Henry VIII's Master of the Hounds, as the Tudor Monarch had hunted nearby. He was granted a royal licence by the Crown to sell refreshments to passing travellers and The Spotted Dog was born, utilising an existing timber barn building.

While it has been modified and extended many times in the nigh on 500 years since then, aspects of the original building still exist and are acknowledged in the official Grade II listing of the building from 1967, with the central range of the main frontage dated back to the late fifteenth or early sixteenth century. It was used by London's merchants as a trading point at the start of the seventeenth century when they were escaping the plague-ridden capital and again when the disease struck in 1665. It was also referenced in Daniel Defoe's *History of the Plague in London* as a place where Londoners more generally came to escape the city, given the fact the pub was surrounded by fields.

In time the urban area of Essex expanded to reach the pub and then as administrative boundaries were redrawn, it found itself part of Greater London from 1965. The author of the London Shoes website recalls visiting the pub in the early 1970s as a young teenager before going to West Ham games, as it was a more sedate spot than the pubs closer to the ground and he was also more likely to get served!

It closed its doors in 2004 but thanks to its listing and historic status, the building is still standing. It is however in a perilous condition and in 2009 the London Fire Brigade stated it was now a dangerous structure.

There has been a concerted effort to save this piece of London's history with an active local campaign group. In 2020 Newham Council granted planning permission for an adjacent hotel development which would also include the restoration of the pub, so there could yet be life in the old dog yet.

THE OLD WHITE HORSE

Ockendon Road, RM14 3PT

This was a landmark London pub, closest to the capital's eastern boundary with Essex. Records state there had been a pub here since at least 1826, although the building certainly looks as if it's been rebuilt at least once since then.

I visited in July 2016 at the end of a pub crawl I did for *Londonist*, visiting the pubs closest to London's southern, western, northern and eastern boundaries. With its huge back garden which you can see in the photo on the previous page and location by various farmers' fields, it definitely felt much more like a village pub. The interior was also suitably traditional, with old adverts for Bovril on the wall.

It was also located in the section of Ockendon beyond the M25, that small part of London that is outside the boundary set by the notorious ring road.

The Google reviews here were largely positive with a 4.7 out of 5 generated by 367 users.

The pub survived the tumultuous times of covid only to close suddenly in Autumn 2022. There have been no plans brought forward yet for the building.

THE POMPADOURS

105 Hilldene Avenue, RM3 8YL

Any ex-pub with a unique name naturally jumped out at me while researching this book – I'm glad this one did as it has a colourful history. It opened in 1959 with the name chosen by public vote, Pompadour being the nickname of a local Essex regiment, who in turn gained that name because of the purple on their uniforms, the shade being the favourite colour of French figure Madame De Pompadour.

In early 2015 the pub was threatened with closure, which led the *Romford Recorder* to do a retrospective piece on the Pomp. In this article they revealed that during the 1970s it went through seventeen managers in three years – giving Watford FC of recent years a run for their money – as it was so hard to manage. A local historian Don Tait even recalled a time where the incumbent just walked out and left the pub open and bar unguarded. Apparently the free bar continued for two days before the police came to lock it up. Tait went on to say that the pub was much better than it had been and he'd be sad to see it go.

A blogger who used to live in the area stated the pub had a nickname during the 1980s and '90s of the Flying Bottles due to the fighting that occurred here, something he said that got worse once a pool table was installed and many of the regulars started using the cues in their arguments.

It closed in March 2016. There were fires in the derelict building later that year which were thought to be caused by squatters but this wasn't confirmed. A planning application to demolish the pub and replace it with twenty-one homes was approved by Havering Council in February 2021.

RAILWAY HOTEL/CUNDY'S

2 Connaught Road, E16 2DB

In its early days this pub played a pivotal role in the establishment of the modern Trade Union movement in London. In 1889 it hosted events for the striking workers at the nearby Silver's India Rubber, Gutta Percha and the Telegraph Cable Company.

Eleanor Marx, daughter of Karl, held meetings here in support of the workers and the landlady Mrs Cundy let the pub be used as the strike HQ. While the strike was ultimately unsuccessful, it has been seen as providing an inspiration for others across the country to organise in the same way. In the early part of the twentieth century the pub was renamed Cundy's after the former managers here.

The pub had fallen on hard times by the noughties and featured on the website Dodgy Boozers in July 2007. The summary of the pub (complete with photos to back up the claims) makes for eye opening reading. From every window in the pub being broken and repaired with clingfilm through to seating patched up with gaffer tape(the author guessing tears caused by knife wounds), Cundy's sounded like a pub very much on its last legs.

There were also apparently strippers here in its final days in a bid to drum up custom, but the pub closed in January 2008. It has since been demolished and replaced by a block of silver clad modern flats.

THE ROYAL PAVILION HOTEL

2 Pier Road, E16 2JJ

Occupying a prime spot right by the river, the Royal Pavilion Hotel opened in the 1850s to cash in on travellers making their way into London via the river or recently opened railway. It was also well located for those working in Royal Albert Docks.

It gained an unexpected attraction at the very end of the Victorian era when a giant whale washed up on the shore beside it in 1899. The landlord collected money from sightseers which he donated to The Mansion House fund, a charity appeal run by the Lord Mayor of London.

In the post-war period it was a popular place for live music and in particular jazz. In the *Romance of Thames-Side Taverns* Glyn Morgan praised the pub's outside terrace looking onto the river as a 'place to sit, to stare, and sometimes to think'. The exterior also featured a large neon sign for Courage beer (as seen in the photo on the next page) which was visible on the other side of the river. The pub and sign also make a brief cameo in the 1987 film *A Prayer for The Dying*.

The Docks closed in 1981 but the pub was still going into the 1990s and was described in the Nicholson guide as an attractive pub right by the riverside, 'a traditional East End family place' complete with a restaurant area serving 'simple, home cooked meals'.

The pub closed in 2000 and was demolished two years later, with flats built on the site some years afterwards.

THE TWO PUDDINGS

27 The Broadway, E15 4BQ

This first began life as The Refreshment Room, had a spell as The Wheatsheaf but it was as The Two Puddings it entered into east London folklore.

It acquired the nickname of 'The Butcher's Shop' on account of the blood spilt here. From 1962 it came under the stewardship of Eddie Johnson. In 2012 he wrote a memoir of his time here during the 1960s called *Tales from the Two Puddings* which was adapted into a documentary film four years later. In this Johnson captured how it played a pivotal role in '60s Stratford life. The book covers both his recollection of the famous visitors, such as Harry Redknapp meeting his wife here, as well as the local characters that enlivened his time in charge. Johnson also told the story that Jack Charlton apparently ended up here at some point after England's World Cup victory in 1966. Johnson himself wasn't here to witness this and when he later met Charlton and asked him, the big man said he didn't remember but that it was entirely possible!

The Puddings closed in 2000 as Eddie's thirty-eight-year tenure at the helm came to an end. For the next two decades it traded under a variety of different names such as Swagga and, demonstrating the circular nature of life, The Refreshment Room, its last guise before closing. The website from that era is still online and states that it was a rum bar.

THE WHITE HART

Collier Row Road, RM5 2BE

First opened in 1896, this cavernous pub established itself as a firm favourite on the Romford pub scene.

The pub had a spell called Double Top when it was owned by the five-time darts champion Eric Bristow and was suitably themed towards his former sport. He wasn't a hands-off presence either as locals recall seeing him at the oche during his time here.

The vast pub had room to accommodate a kids' play area complete with ball pit. This was remembered particularly fondly in a *Romford Recorder* article both from those who recalled being taken here as children and treated to turkey dinosaurs here afterwards, as well as the parents who looked back nostalgically at having somewhere for their kids to let off steam while they had a cheeky shandy.

The pub closed in 2006 and was demolished to be replaced by a block of retirement flats called Tithe Court.

HAMMERSMITH & FULHAM AND HOUNSLOW

BRITANNIA TAP

150 Warwick Road, W14 8PS

Once claiming to be London's smallest pub with a bar area of only 200 square feet, this late nineteenth century establishment eventually ended up generating so much interest from people wanting to see it for themselves that the owners Young's decided to expand it.

The larger Britannia was opened on 7 October 1969 by the head of the brewery himself, John Young. The extension generated a fair bit of press coverage reflecting on the irony of expanding to accommodate the extra crowd who'd come to see London's smallest pub, but in the process removing that accolade!

The other interesting quirk of the Britannia is that it sat a few doors away from a Fuller's pub, The Warwick, the closest that these two London powerhouse breweries ever had their pubs.

The Britannia closed in 2011 and was converted into housing, leaving The Warwick without its friendly rival.

THE BRICKLAYERS ARMS

67 Ealing Road, TW8 0LQ

The Bricklayers first opened in 1853. By the start of the 1960s it was a popular venue for live jazz, including by a band called The Temperance Seven who went on to have chart success in the first half of the decade and were known for their surreal performances.

The musical theme continued well into the 1980s and '90s. Given its proximity to Griffin Park, it was also very popular with Brentford fans on matchdays and even of players of theirs. Former landlord Ken Martin told me that cult player Stan Bowles was a regular here.

Talking of cult, the Bricklayers also made it into the world of fantasy as it was used as the inspiration for the Flying Swan in Robert Rankin's series of books on Brentford. Rankin, a Brentford fan, was known to visit the pub on matchdays.

The pub made it into the new millennium but bowed out in 2009 when it was converted into houses. The top of the building still proudly proclaims it's the Bricklayers Arms, something you can get a good view of from the top deck of the 65 bus.

THE CLEM ATTLEE

99 Rylston Road, SW6 7HP

While London has a few pubs named after wartime Prime Minister Winston Churchill, there are none named after the man who defeated him with a landslide in 1945, Clement Attlee. This wasn't always the case and in 1971 a new pub named after the PM who presided over the introduction of the NHS opened on Rylston Road, adjacent to an estate also named after Attlee.

The brewery even got his son in, Earl Attlee, for the official opening in April 1971. It rarely appeared in London pub guides and when it did appear in Martin Green's title from 1982, the author managed to combine a slight against both pub and man when commenting that the pub is 'decorated with pictures and cartoons of the unassuming Labour leader' then following it up by saying the pub had 'as much personality' as the 1945 general election victor.

It later had a stint as The Pump House before becoming Paya and Horse, an English pub with a Serbian twist for a few years by the mid-2000s. The Horse bolted south of the river in 2007 and can now be found residing in Battersea while the building here was demolished in 2011.

COACH AND HORSES

25–29 Chiswick High Road, W4 2ND

This book includes various theme pubs back from back in the day but here we have London's only ever 'stream' pub!

Tracing its history back to the eighteenth century, the Coach and Horses was rebuilt at the start of the twentieth century in an impressive manner. In the 1970s it was rebranded as The Schooner Inn, promoted as the only pub to have a stream running through it. During this period the pub's exterior was decorated in a garish pink colour scheme which caused enough complaints that it was quickly dropped. This wasn't the end to bold statements on this corner of Chiswick High Road. They also had a large horse drawn carriage on their first-floor balcony, as opposed to having a typical pub sign.

In the 1990s and 2000s the use of the building flitted between a variety of bars and restaurants, none of these with a stream sadly. In 2012 the building was demolished yet replaced with one that was, on the exterior at least, an exact replica of the original. It does beg the question as to why they demolished it in the first place.

THE GENERAL SMUTS

95 Bloemfontein Road, W12 7DA

Given it took fifteen years for The General Smuts to be built, it feels a waste that it has now shut down. Construction began alongside the creation of the new White City Estate in 1937, halted due to the war and was only eventually completed in 1952.

The name was chosen in 1937, Smuts being General Jan Smuts, South African Prime Minister over two periods between 1919 and 1948, carrying on the South African theme established with the name of the street it was located on, Bloemfontein Road.

With its close proximity to Loftus Road, it quickly became known as a firm favourite for QPR fans. It is another former pub that pops up in Robert Elms' autobiography *London Made Us*, where he nostalgically recalls having to find his Grandad in there and get him home for Sunday lunch.

In its later years it acquired an increasingly unsavoury reputation and was associated with football hooliganism and crime more generally. Warnings from the Council and Police were not acted upon and in 2011 the licence was revoked, the chair of the licensing committee stating in the press release that they'd called 'last orders' on the pub. Media stories written at the time picked up on an online review of the pub which called it 'supremely scary' and served as its epitaph. The building was divided up with part becoming the Egyptian Lounge restaurant and unbelievably another becoming Smuts Bar, in some sort of impressive afterlife for the General. This only lasted a few years before closing in 2015. The Egyptian Lounge is now called the Sphinx Lounge whereas Smuts Bar is now an Islamic Prayer Centre, overcoming the issues encountered ten years previously.

GOLDEN GLOVES/OLD SUFFOLK PUNCH

80 Fulham Palace Road, W6 9PL

Back in the day this place used to land a knockout blow. Beginning life in the 1850s as The Rifle, a century on it was rechristened The Golden Gloves and entered its heavyweight era. Owned by the Mancini brothers, it became a pub paying homage to boxing, Tony Mancini being a professional boxer. It was filled with boxing memorabilia and even featured a scarlet carpet with a golden glove motif. It was both a popular venue for boxing matches and then a haven for live music by the 1980s.

The Mancinis' long stint in the pub came to an end in the 1990s and it was renamed as the Old Suffolk Punch. It then had a stint as a modern bar called the OSP which was described online as 'an awful, soul-destroying place' featuring 'light box murals' of grinning young people having a great time. It was the Old Suffolk Punch again by the end of the noughties under the stewardship of Greene King.

It changed hands again towards the tail end of the 2010s as it was taken over by Maverick Pubs who are owned by the West Berkshire Brewery Company. This venture did not reopen after the pandemic and in January 2023 a planning application was approved which would see the original building demolished and replaced with a hotel which should include a pub on the ground floor. We'll keep our eyes peeled!

THE HOPE AND ANCHOR

20 Macbeth Street, W6 9JJ

This Grade II listed building dates from 1936, and was built by the brewery Trumans at the same time as a neighbouring housing estate.

It featured in the 2006 edition of the *Time Out* guide where it was called an 'old fashioned boozer' which the reviewer felt had avoided being turned into a gastropub and could offer darts, pool and 'a good crew of venerable regulars'.

The Hope shut its doors in 2012 but the interior has been retained and is now used as a film set, its most high-profile appearance being in *The Crown*. The pub's listing document by Historic England highlights the 'exceptionally intact 1930s bar interior' and picks it out as an unusual survivor from this era.

THE KING'S HEAD

4 Fulham High Street, SW6 3LQ

This early Edwardian imposing building dates back to 1906, complete with its own impressive turret, and was Grade II listed in 1985.

It long had a reputation for live music and certainly had the space to keep the gigs separate from the main bar area. In 1995 the *Evening Standard* guide spilled the beans on how it was now according to the pub's manager 'No.1 for secret gigs', with the entry going on to list recent acts performing here including Robert Plant and Paul Young. By the end of the decade the final edition of the *Standard's* guide explained that punters could bring their own food like sausages and burgers to put on the pub's barbecue in the large beer garden. Other online sources I've seen suggested this garden could accommodate up to 400 people.

From the early 2000s it cycled through a variety of different identities including such snappily named ventures as Ox Wagon, Joe Cool's and Zulu's. Its most recent incarnation was Courtyard, reflecting both the size of the beer garden and also a nod to the original name.

The portcullis went down on the Courtyard at the start of 2020 and the main part of the building remains unoccupied, although part of the ground floor is now a martial arts centre.

THE MAILCOACH

28 Uxbridge Road, W12 8LH

This pub first opened in 1932 and was designed by the architect Alfred W. Blomfield, who was also responsible for some notable London pubs such as the Bedford in Balham, the French House in Soho and the Dagenham Roundhouse, the latter being my favourite of the three.

The Mailcoach was decorated with various items of transport memorabilia, which was in keeping with the fact it was popular with Underground staff working at the nearby Shepherd's Bush station.

When the plans for the Westfield shopping centre were first announced, The Mailcoach was originally going to be spared the wrecking ball in the original 2000 planning application. However the revised application submitted in 2003 had it within the area being cleared.

It closed the same year and ironically the site is now occupied by another form of transport, namely the bus station outside Westfield.

THE MAWSONS ARMS/THE FOX AND HOUNDS

110 Chiswick Lane South, W4 2QA

When this pub adjoining the Griffin brewery shut down in 2020, London lost the curiosity of a pub with two names.

It first opened in 1759 as The Mawson Arms, commemorating the Mawson family as earlier owners of the Griffin Brewery. When the neighbouring Fox and Hounds pub was extended, the two pubs were joined together as one but retained two separate names. This would give anyone travelling along the A4 a curious sight as depending on what part of the building you looked at, you'd see a different name!

Before it became a pub the building was at one point home to the poet Alexander Pope, who in an interesting twist of fate has a pub named after him in Twickenham which is owned by Fuller's long-time London rivals (in the friendliest sense) Young's. In the latter years of the pub Fuller's also named a private dining room upstairs here after Pope.

The pub was open right up until the March 2020 lockdown but its permanent closure was confirmed in July 2020. This was due to the sale of Fuller's brewing arm to the Japanese brewery Asahi, with the ongoing Fuller's business which continued to own the company's pub estate deciding to sell up. A Fuller's pub still remains trading, a three minute walk away at the George and Devonshire and I am sympathetic to the challenges of keeping two pubs afloat right by the Great West Road.

THE OLD PARR'S HEAD

120 Blythe Road, W14 0HD

First opened as the Duke of Edinburgh in 1867, it was renamed four years later after Thomas Parr, another pub named after that grand old man.

This sidestreet pub near Kensington Olympia had a brush with fame in the 1980s when it popped up in episodes of the ITV classic sitcom, *Minder*. In one storyline the landlord of the pub even gives a key bit of information to Terry (Dennis Waterman's character) which helps him track down some vandals who have been causing trouble in the local area.

From 1990 to 2013 it was run by Joe and Betty Hynes, establishing a reputation as a popular locals' pub and even popping up in the 2003 Harden's Bar and Pub

Guide, where it was praised for providing 'good, cheap Thai scoff in a cosy pub environment'.

The pub didn't last long after the Hynes retired, closing less than six months later. An initial application for a residential conversion was turned down by Hammersmith and Fulham Council but granted on appeal by the planning inspectorate in 2016.

THE POTTERY ARMS

25 Clayponds Lane, TW8 0BN

Another pub designed by the prolific T.H. Nowell Parr, the present building dates from 1927, replacing the earlier structure which had been here since 1888. Brentford is home to a host of buildings designed by Parr, from other pubs like the distinctive gold dome topped Beehive but also civic buildings such as Brentford Library and my own personal favourite, the red brick former fire station which is now in use as a restaurant.

There was lots of upheaval in Brentford in the 1960s and '70s and the pub narrowly avoided demolition in 1971. Mary Tilling, who worked here as a barmaid in the 1980s, told me it was a busy place then, with lots of lunchtime trade from workers at the nearby Beecham offices. CAMRA's *West London Pub Guide* remarked in 2005 that the pub had perked up a bit after a recent rough spell and was popular with football fans and local workers.

The pub closed in 2008 and was converted into housing. Much of the pub's external features were retained, including the tiling and pub sign. I walked past on numerous occasions during lockdown walks of 2020/21 which always left me wondering what the pub must have been like.

THE PRINCESS ROYAL

107 Ealing Road, TW8 0LF

Appropriately enough for a football ground named after a pub, Brentford's Griffin Park was famous for having a pub on each corner of the ground.

The Princess Royal was located on the south-eastern side of the ground, backing onto Ealing Road. The pub first opened in 1841 with the current building dating from 1924 and being yet another offering from the T.H. Nowell Parr portfolio.

The pub formed part of the Fuller's estate apart from a brief period from 2005–2010 when the club ran it themselves. It closed for lockdown 2020 and never reopened. By the time restrictions had been lifted Brentford had played their last match to fans at Griffin Park and without that lucrative source of trade every other Saturday for half of the year, Fuller's put the place up for sale.

It was rumoured that Tesco and Sainsbury's were both vying for the site but ultimately it ended up changing hands for over £1.2 million and was acquired by the Armenian Church in the UK. The conversion of the building into both an HQ and prayer and study space for the church was completed in the summer of 2023.

The three pubs on the other corners of the ground are still trading, as is the Royal Guardsman which is only a couple of minutes south of the Princess Royal. So rest easy, you can still do a four-stop pub crawl around the site of Griffin Park if you're that way inclined.

RAVENSCOURT ARMS/BLACK BULL

257 King Street, W6 9LU

This flat roof pub first opened on 12 July 1966, in a ceremony presided over by the then Mayor, Cllr L.W. Freeman. It replaced a previous Ravenscourt Arms which was demolished as part of the widening of King Street in the first half of the sixties. In 2004 Chris Amies remarked that it was 'much frequented by people from Waterford, Ireland'.

In its final years before it closed down in 2018, the pub was renamed after the statue of the Black Bull which still stands outside the derelict structure today. This bovine sculpture has moved around a bit in its time, having initially grazed outside the Black Bull Inn in High Holborn, an establishment mentioned in Charles Dickens' *Martin Chuzzlewit*. When that pub was demolished in 1904 the Bull was saved by Hammersmith's then MP, Sir William Bull, who had it transported to the outside of the offices of a firm of solicitors called Bull and Bull, where it sat above the main entrance to the building. In the 1960s that building was also demolished and the bull ended up here. If this old pub also eventually goes the same way then who knows where this plucky adventurer may eventually end up. The Hammersmith Society and the Heritage of London Trust are keen to see the bull restored and find a new home, so there are some people trying to secure him his next home.

THE SEVEN STARS

253 North End Road, W14 9NS

This Art Deco delight was designed by John Nowell Parr, son of T.H. Nowell Parr who has been very well represented in this book. With this fine building which from certain angles is reminiscent of the best type of 1930s railway architecture, John clearly proved himself to be a chip off the old block.

The building dates from 1938, replacing an earlier Seven Stars in the same area. This was a Fuller's pub for the duration of its life. In a 2006 review from the *Fancyapint?* guide, it was described as having a lot of wood panelling giving it a 'clubby/parlour' atmosphere, although this was contrasted by there also being disco lights and DJs and karaoke here at weekends. For the more cerebral minded, there was chess on Wednesdays.

Fuller's sold up in 2009 with the pub closed the following year. Property developers then converted it into student flats, which were described as 'offering a new standard of luxury student housing'.

OUTER WEST (BRENT, EALING, HILLINGDON)

THE ANGEL

697 Uxbridge Road, UB4 8HX

Opened in 1926, this is yet another pub designed by T.H. Nowell Parr for Fuller's, this being the most westerly of his pub portfolio in the early twentieth century.

This expansive roadhouse pub was considered part of the 'Improved House' movement, an attempt by breweries to demonstrate that pubs were not merely small dens of iniquity where people could drink themselves silly but well-appointed buildings with a whole host of facilities. They were particularly well suited to the expanding London suburbia, both in terms of the additional space available but also to demonstrate a clean break with the past to persuade wary local magistrates to grant a licence.

The pub was divided up into four bars and even had an Art Deco masonic lodge in its first-floor club room. A CAMRA inventory of the pub from the early 2010s noted how little had been altered in the pub, this they linked to the fact there had been the same landlord here for over 40 years. There were a variety of events that took place here, from comedy through to jazz and film nights. The pub was also in both the local darts and pool leagues.

English Heritage recognised the importance of the pub in 2015 by awarding it a Grade II listing. Three years later Fuller's sold the pub and it was bought by the Hayes Muslim Centre. However their application for its conversion to a community centre was rejected. The building presently lies empty with its future uncertain.

BIDDY MULLIGAN'S

205 Kilburn High Road, NW6 7HY

This started life as The Victoria Tavern in the early 1860s before being renamed as Biddy Mulligan's in 1971.

The *Evening Standard* pub guide published two years later called it London's first 'Orish' pub, describing an interior mocked up to look like a 'West Cork Tithe

Barne', including pillars disguised as trees alongside stone walls and fireplaces. The name itself came from a drag act of a popular Irish comedian, Jimmy O'Dea, with Mulligan being a Dublin street seller.

The pub was popular with the Irish residents of Kilburn and it was reported that collections were made for the IRA here, something the novelist Zadie Smith mentions witnessing in the pub when she was taken there by her mother in this period. In December 1975 it was targeted in a bomb attack by the loyalist Ulster Defence Association, due to the fact it was frequented by Republican sympathisers and the fundraising efforts here. Thankfully nobody was killed and four men were jailed for the attack the following year.

These events were not mentioned in its entry in Martin Green's 1982 *London Pub Guide* (the text largely being lifted from his 1973 edition under the *Evening Standard* banner) nor eight years later in the Nicholson guide. The latter referred to it feeling 'a bit like drinking in someone's house' here as well as the smell of 'Irish stews waft from the kitchen'. Given the charged political environment during the era of the Troubles, I can understand why books marketed towards tourists might not want to dwell on the incident.

In its later years the name was shortened to simply Biddys and in its final days it was known as Southern K. The shutters had come down for good by the end of 2007 and the building is now in use as a Ladbrokes.

THE CASTLE

140 Victoria Road, W3 6UL

This Castle first emerged from the battlements in 1924, built to take advantage of the arrival of the new North Acton tube station. Its location near former BBC rehearsal studios meant it was once common to see radio and TV stars popping in here for a drink and the pub used to mark this with signed photos of some of the leading lights on the wall.

I first visited The Castle in 2015 when doing my blog INNsidetrack. At the time major large-scale new developments were springing up all around the tube station (including a significant mass of buildings for Imperial College) and The Castle with its arts and crafts exterior felt like the odd one out in the nicest possible way. My friend and I were both fans of the pub as a solid unfussy Fuller's offering. The signed photos were gone but I was taken with the collage of 1980s football magazines that surrounded one of the TVs.

Plans for the levelling of The Castle and its replacement with high rise towers emerged in the latter part of the last decade. A local campaign started to save the pub but it closed for good in Autumn 2020 before the start of the second lockdown. Ealing Council granted planning approval for two towers, at thirty-two and twenty-seven storeys apiece, in September 2022. Final approval was confirmed by the GLA in May 2023 with the developers also promising a new pub as a focal point of the development. In a local news article, a spokesperson for the developers Tide explained that the pub will contain 'a sculptural elevation that pays homage to the architecture of everyday London pubs'. One to look out for in due course.

HAMBROUGH TAVERN

The Broadway, UB1 1NG

This pub found itself at the epicentre of a race riot in 1981 where it was burnt to the ground before eventually being rebuilt. On Friday 3 July 1981 several bands from the 'Oi!' movement were set to play a gig at the pub. The movement itself was not overtly racist but the events did attract skinheads and those with neo-Nazi tendencies.

Some of the mob going to the gig had been breaking shop windows and abusing residents in this predominantly Asian area. This caused members of the local community to come out on the street to fight back and the ensuing confrontation saw a petrol bomb thrown at the pub which razed it to the ground.

The pub, which had first opened in the 1870s, was duly rebuilt and became a shrine for the Asian community in the words of local ward councillor Shambhu Gupta. The new building was a fairly modest flat roof affair.

The Hambrough closed just before the covid pandemic. Planning permission was granted for its demolition in 2020 and replacement with a fifteen-storey hotel.

HOG'S GRUNT/MAGIC HOUR

Production Village, 100 Cricklewood Lane, NW2 2DP

In the late 1970s someone had the brainwave of creating a fake village on the edge of the Cricklewood film studios site as an entertainment complex which could also mock up as a film set. Now all villages, fake or otherwise, need a pub and so 'Production Village' as it was called acquired two pubs called the Hog's Grunt and Magic Hour.

The Hog's Grunt was set up like a barn while the Magic Hour was supposed to be akin to a Victorian pub with gas lamps and a log fire. The spiel from the operators of the complex stated it was a 'Village pub in the traditional manner', which also overlooked the duck pond.

Incredibly on 8 January 1982 Freddie Mercury turned up at the Hog and provided the locals with an impromptu performance of *Jailhouse Rock* alongside his friend Peter Straker's band Taxi. A recording is available on YouTube.

As the decade went on, the pubs started to have issues with drugs and violence. Speaking in the late 1990s, Tony Samuelson said how it got to the point where they had metal detectors to check people for weapons. The Samuelsons sold up before the decade was out to Bass Taverns.

The Village fell on hard times during the 1990s and became increasingly run down. The whole thing closed down in 1999 and was demolished soon after and replaced with a gym. The authors of the website London RIP, which focused on lost locations in London, remarked that the whole place had been as 'mad as a box of frogs' and 'utterly unrepeatable'.

THE PADDINGTON PACKET BOAT

High Road, UB8 2HT

Named after a boat which used to take people from here (Uxbridge) down to Paddington via the Grand Union Canal, the pub first opened in 1804. While the role of canals was soon superseded by that of the railway, the Packet Boat remained a fixture here for well over 200 years and was extended towards the end of the nineteenth century.

It was still going strong well into the 2010s, retaining some old memorabilia relating to the boat as well as framed pieces of glass from when the pub was still divided into separate bars. It was a regular venue for live music tribute acts. It also had a handful of hotel rooms upstairs and one of the final reviews of the pub online is from a customer praising the pub after they needed to stay there after their flight was cancelled from nearby Heathrow. A perfect example of all the change that happened while the pub was trading. It began life to serve canal boat passengers

and ended it as a convenient spot to stay before using one of the world's largest airports.

The Boat closed its doors for the last time in September 2018 and was snapped up by a property developer. While the building was never listed, Hillingdon Council had placed it on their local listing (not binding), with an entry that included references to it being a 'landmark corner building' and having 'strong community value'. Despite this, the application for its demolition and replacement with student accommodation was granted in November 2022.

THE QUEENSBURY

110a Walm Lane, NW2 4RS

The building that eventually housed The Queensbury started life as a doctor's surgery. It was then converted into a Conservative Club before becoming a pub. It was called The Green for a spell before becoming the Queensbury in the late noughties when it was refurbished into a gastropub.

In 2012 the building was sold to property developers Fairview Homes Limited who had designs on putting fifty-six homes on the site. A campaign to save the pub quickly emerged and by the end of the year it included the pop band The Wanted alongside former Mayor of London and Cricklewood resident Ken Livingstone.

I visited in mid-2013 as one of the early stops on my blog INNside Track, with the Queensbury standing out as a welcoming community pub on a stretch of the

Jubilee Line not particularly blessed with good drinking options. What was also interesting was the variety of uses for the pub, including a parent and baby club during the week called the Busy Rascals. While to some this might feel a million miles away from the traditional idea of a pub, to me it was a brilliant illustration of a venue adapting its role while staying at the heart of its community.

The initial application for housing on the site was unsuccessful, as was the appeal, but the developers worked on the maxim of 'If at first you don't succeed…' and when a follow-up application was also refused, appealed again and this time the planning inspectorate granted approval in November 2019.

The pub then soldiered on for a bit, opening up after covid lockdowns, before finally closing for good in April 2023. Demolition of the old building commenced in autumn 2023. There has been the promise of a new pub on the ground floor of the development but only time will tell if it materialises.

THREE HORSESHOES

2 High Street, UB1 3DA

In its prime this occupied a key location in the centre of Southall. Originally planned in 1914 but not completed until 1922 due in part to the impact of the First World War, this was designed by T.H. Nowell Parr. In their excellent book looking at pubs and pub culture in the twentieth century, Jessica Boak and Ray Bailey identified this as one of the first examples of a style which became known as 'Brewers Tudor'.

The pub's time was nearly cut short in 1989 when a proposal by Ealing Council to redevelop Southall town centre would have seen the building demolished. This provoked a wave of opposition not only from CAMRA but other organisations such as English Heritage who looked to have the building listed. Ealing were able to successfully have the listing overturned on a technicality that as the building was completed after the First World War, it should be subject to the more rigorous listing criteria than if it had dated from 1914 when the project started.

In the end the plans for Southall were shelved by the council, in part due to the recession of the early 1990s, and the pub lived to fight another day. It was also apparently at risk due to the West London Tram proposal, an idea that was mooted in the first days of TfL in the early noughties but dropped following significant local opposition.

The bell finally rang for the pub in December 2016. The building has at least been retained, albeit converted into flats and shops, which is preferable to it being flattened.

OUTER NORTH (BARNET, ENFIELD, HARROW)

THE BALD FACED STAG

104 Burnt Oak Broadway, H8 0BE

The first Stag came on the scene here in the early nineteenth century and was rebuilt again twice with its last incarnation dating from the 1930s, not long after the Northern Line arrived here in 1924 alongside the development of significant housing estates on what was previously open farmland.

The writer and broadcaster Robert Elms grew up in Burnt Oak in the 1960s and '70s and described the Bald Faced Stag in his book *London Made Us* as 'a boozer so wantonly wild it was an entertainment in itself', explaining how it wasn't uncommon for the regulars to lock the landlord in the cupboard and help themselves to the drinks, as well as drunken duels taking place in the car park with chair legs.

Pete Scully, who originally hailed from Burnt Oak, drew the pub for his sketch blog in November 2009 and wrote how there was a sign outside the pub that said 'Please Beware, This is the Bald Faced Stag'. One of the last online reviews for the pub from 2010 was particularly scathing, calling it a 'complete dump' with punters that would look more at home in a 'house of horrors'. The Stag didn't survive much longer and closed in 2012. It ended up as a furniture shop for a few years before being demolished in 2018 and replaced with housing.

THE CASE IS ALTERED

Old Redding, HA3 6SE

At one point there were three pubs across the borough of Harrow all with this distinctive name. This 'case' first opened at the turn of the nineteenth century and was located in a converted cottage on the approach to Grim's Dyke House.

Various theories have been put forward for why Harrow ended up with multiple altered cases. One that has been cited by many (including in a letter to *The Independent* in 2002) but was labelled as almost certainly false in *The Wordsworth Dictionary of Pub Names* is that it was a corruption of the Spanish term 'Casa

Alta' due to soldiers from the nearby Middlesex regiment returning to the local area after the Peninsula War at the start of the 1800s and who had often occupied a house on the hill (casa alta meaning high house) during battles, and had brought the name back with them. The less exciting but more conventionally accepted origin is that it became popular from the proverb that sprung up from the sixteenth century after being first uttered by the lawyer Edward Plowden when responding to new evidence during the proceedings of a case. It then in turn became the title of a play by Ben Johnson in 1609.

It was blessed with a brief mention in the seminal 1971 book *Nairn's London*, penned by the architectural writer Ian Nairn, where there is a wider piece on Grim's Dyke House but he did call The Case 'a proper country pub'.

In a review carried in the *Watford Observer* in 2002, the writer began by sharing a reflection on the pub which ultimately was to be its undoing. The Case was located next to the Old Redding municipal car park, a handy point for people starting a scenic panoramic circular walk. However the review alluded to its other source of popularity, saying it was 'legendary among courting couples' and in a very colourful turn of phrase, had 'seen more action than John Motson's sheepskin'.

Those may have been more benign times but by the late 2010s the car park was under fire from Harrow Council as an anti-social behaviour hotspot including reckless driving through to drug taking, fights and dogging. In late 2019 the council ordered the car park to shut at 6pm each evening, something the pub protested at, given their rural location. There then followed a period where the car park was open on an 'on-off' basis and latterly restricted to merely being open 8am–4pm.

In its final days the pub too ended up curtailing its opening hours to a mere four hours a day, 12–4pm. This was clearly going to be an unviable proposition and it closed for good in March 2022. The pub's final owners hit out at Harrow Council via *The Harrow Times* saying there were ways the issue could have been sorted without the strict restrictions on the car park. The then leader of the Council hit back by saying they'd offered the pub solutions such as shared security management of the car park but the pub had been unwilling to take them forward. Ironically another explanation for the name 'Case is Altered' is where a licensee had encountered problems with the local licensing authority, something that certainly rings true here!

THE FALLOW BUCK

Clay Hill, EN2 9JD

Perched on Clay Hill, the Fallow Buck was once one of the most northerly pubs in Greater London.

A Grade II listed building since 1974, the listing states parts of the building dates as back as far as the seventeenth century. From old photos online it certainly looked every bit the classic country pub with its painted pine weatherboarded exterior. The pub closed in 2013 and was converted into residential use.

When it was put up for sale in 2020 for £1.5 million, a local Enfield news site gushed over it as a 'stunning house', alongside ten photos of the well-equipped property and its spacious and multiple gardens.

THE GREEN DRAGON

889 Green Lanes, N21 2QP

An Enfield landmark, the Green Dragon sat watching over this spot in north London for well over 270 years. Thought to date back to 1730, the pub was modified several times over the years, the most recent being during the 1930s where it picked up the 'Brewers Tudor' look that was doing the rounds at that point.

In 1999 it became part of the Jim Thompson chain of Asian restaurants which were fairly commonplace in London for a time. In 2015 it was acquired by the company Green Lanes Development who announced plans to convert the pub into a supermarket. A strong community campaign was launched to save the pub but they were unable to get Enfield Council to list it as an ACV to stall the developers, and planning approval for the conversion was issued in 2016. It is now a Waitrose.

The Green Dragon name still lives on within the Enfield community though. Two years after the pub closed, local resident Richard Reeves opened the Green Dragon Micropub, having spent 2015 visiting all 100 micropubs in the UK for charity. I am happy to report the micro Dragon is thriving!

JACK STRAW'S CASTLE

North End Way, NW3 7ES

Arguably the most famous of the former pubs featured within this book, the first pub here dated back to the early eighteenth century. The building was badly damaged during the blitz and was replaced with a new structure which opened in 1964 and was designed by Raymond Erith. This building was listed in 1994, the soonest that accreditation is permissible under the rules governing these awards.

It took its name from one of the leaders of the Peasants' Revolt in 1381 who hid nearby for a spell until being caught and executed. It also boasts an impressive literary heritage, with both Charles Dickens and William Thackeray being known to frequent it, as well as featuring in Bram Stoker's *Dracula.* Dickens was said to have had a fondness for the 'red hot' chops you could buy here.

The start of the millennium brought grim tidings for this venerable Hampstead institution. In late 2000 it was snapped up by a property developer and closed as a pub a few months later. During a period of inertia while future plans for the pub were being squabbled over, the state of the Grade II listed building deteriorated to the extent it was included in the 2002 edition of English Heritage's 'At Risk' register. A conversion into private flats with a ground floor space reserved for a pub restaurant was completed by 2003, the occasion marked by a visit of its famous namesake, Jack Straw MP, then Foreign Secretary. The pub restaurant never came and this prime position for a pub remains unfulfilled.

As famous London pubs go, it's right up there, and it featured in every single one of the various books I looked through about London pubs that were published from the 1960s right through to 2000. While the name might still be proudly displayed on its frontage, the doors remain resolutely shut to anyone fancying a pint.

THE KING'S HEAD HOTEL

88 High Street, HA1 3LW

There are claims this pub's lineage goes back to the sixteenth century and was a hunting lodge of Henry VIII, incidentally not the only pub within these pages to have claimed this! The present building dates from the eighteenth century and was Grade II listed in 1973.

The pub hit the headlines that same year when a local feminist group tried to demand entry to a bar within the pub (there were three separate areas) which was reserved solely for men. When quoted in a local newspaper, Sally Hale said that she was told by staff that the tradition of this bar dated back to the time of Henry VIII, 'and if we wanted to know why, we would have to ask him.' He probably wanted somewhere to avoid running into an ex-wife or being tempted to marry another one…

This policy was invoked as a reason that the pub should have its licence withdrawn later that year but the local magistrates found in favour of the pub. A spokesman for the brewery was quoted in the same news article as saying 'The situation in this hotel has existed since time immemorial'. Just to add even more historical colour to proceedings, the news article also threw in that Churchill used to drink here too.

Aside from all the controversy, it was a regular in CAMRA's *Good Beer Guide* throughout the 1980s and was praised for having a decent range of ales. The pub closed down in 2001 and the building has been converted into a mixture of apartments and other uses, such as a dentist. There is still a pub sign, with Henry VIII on it naturally, hanging from a gantry on a patch of grass just opposite the building. The gantry is a modern replica, put up in 2013, and has been designed to be more sympathetic to the original than the last one that had been installed in the 1980s.

THE PLOUGH

105 Turkey Street, EN1 4NR

This historic Enfield pub was taken out in a particularly cruel and underhand manner. With suggestions it was up to 400 years old, it had been a fixture in the local area for centuries and was well loved in the community.

It closed abruptly early in the new millennium when the owners, the Laurel Pub Company, sold it to property developer Fairview Homes. Plans were announced for its demolition and replacement with housing. Given the age of the building, English Heritage were planning a visit here to check its suitability for listing. In July 2002, the day before they were due to inspect the building, Fairview sent in the wrecking ball, reminiscent of a pub version of what happened to the Art Deco Firestone factory in Brentford.

The consequences for Fairview were minimal: they were issued with a meagre £500 fine with additional costs of £490 which I'm sure barely touched the sides for them. Residents who'd campaigned to save the pub were suitably unimpressed, telling the local media it wouldn't act as an deterrent at all.

You'd hope these days there would be a more robust response, along the lines of when developers were mandated to rebuild the illegally demolished Carlton Tavern in Maida Vale.

THE RAILWAY HOTEL

40 Station Road, HA8 7AD

This imposing interwar pub first opened in 1932 and again was another example of the 'Brewers Tudor' design. It was named after the old Edgware railway station that was located nearby that closed in the 1960s as opposed to the tube station which opened in the 1920s.

The pub was Grade II listed in 2003 but closed down three years later. What has followed since is a cycle of misfortune for the poor old building. In 2011 its deteriorating condition saw it placed on English Heritage's 'At Risk' register but worse was to come. In 2016 it was hit by a fire which caused significant damage.

Restoration plans were then announced for the stricken structure, including its revival as a hotel. In the meantime, a coach company was using the pub's old car park for their own purposes without permission. Disaster struck again as the pub was hit by another fire in late 2018 which burnt out the roof and left the building exposed to the elements.

Incredibly the pub was then hit by another blaze in September 2021 which saw six fire engines dispatched, with damage sustained on the first floor. By 2023 the building was said to be in severe danger of irreparable damage and that May Barnet Council voted to issue a Compulsory Purchase Order to acquire the pub. The Council plans to restore the building as part of a wider masterplan for Barnet High Street, but the exact use for this grand but unlucky structure has not yet been confirmed.

THE VICTORY

6 High Street, Pinner, HA5 5PW

The building which housed The Victory proudly displays the year it was built on its exterior: 1580. The impressive longevity is not disputed in its Grade II listing which was awarded back in 1951.

Elton John is from Pinner and he famously had a song called *Saturday Night's Alright for Fighting*, but it was on the early hours of a Thursday, New Year's Day 2009, when a brawl kicked off outside the pub. The then landlord Vijay Behl got involved and was said to have punched someone with such force that he sent them crashing to the ground 'like a skittle'. Certainly not the kind of thing I'd associate with Metroland suburbia…

Behl avoided a jail term when it came to court the following year but the incident helped serve as the death knell for the pub which had closed in the months following the incident and which reopened in the summer of 2010 as a branch of the Italian restaurant chain Zizzi.

A row broke out during their tenure here after they disposed of the historic Victory pub sign, which was subsequently found in a skip. It subsequently returned to its rightful place outside the pub. Zizzi's shut the branch around the time of the pandemic. There were then plans to turn it into a Shisha bar which were strongly opposed by the local community, and it became the restaurant Tummies but that has also closed down. The sign has sadly once again disappeared.

WHITE HART HOTEL/CHANGE OF HEART

19–21 High Street, HA8 7EE

A long-time fixture on Edgware High Street, the White Hart Hotel is currently facing an uncertain future but it has beaten the odds before.

The building is commonly thought to date back to the seventeenth century, although a study carried out in 1972 suggested that some of the timber beams may be from as far back as the early 1500s. This information came to light at a time when the pub was under threat as the owners, brewer Ind Coope, wanted to sell it for development as a petrol station and eight storey office block. The plans were unsuccessful, and it received a Grade II listing in 1973, although this made no official reference to the potentially 'medieval' beams that had been referenced in 1972.

The pub had a change of name to the Change of Heart in the 1990s and featured in Peter Haydon's book *Known Treasures and Hidden Gems* from 1996. In this

Haydon praised the owners Allied Danacq for putting in place a 'miraculous transformation' for somewhere that previously looked as if it was being run into the ground but that they had 'brought back from the brink', noting approvingly that he found the pub as somewhere where the only thing to distract from the sound of conversations here was the noise of pints being pulled.

The pub closed in November 2017. It was converted to a restaurant called Dolce LDN which opened in Spring 2019. During the covid lockdown of 2020 unauthorised work was carried out on the building which Harrow Council halted. The Historic England condition report lists these as well as other earlier unauthorised work, which had left the building in a poor condition with holes in the walls and ceilings.

Dolce LDN has not reopened here so the building presently remains derelict and the rather forlorn assessment from Historic England sums it all up really: 'Slow decay, no solution agreed'.

BIBLIOGRAPHY

Nicholson London Pub Guide, Judy Allen, Nicholson Maps, 1987
Nicholson London Pub Guide, Judy Allen, Nicholson Maps, 1990
Nicholson London Pub Guide, Judy Allen, Nicholson Maps, 1995
Hammersmith and Fulham Pubs, Chris Amies, History Press, 2004
Lambeth Architecture 1914-1939, Edmund Bird and Fiona Price, Lambeth Archives and Lambeth Local History Forum, 2012
Lambeth Architecture 1945-65, Edmund Bird and Fiona Price, Lambeth Archives and Lambeth Local History Forum, 2014
20th Century Pub: From Beer House to Booze Bunker, Jessica Boak and Ray Bailey, Homewood Press, 2017
London Heritage Pubs: An Inside Story, Geoff Brandwood and Jane Jephcote, CAMRA Books, 2008
Historic Pubs of London, Ted Bruning, Prion Books, 2001
Brentford and Chiswick Pubs, Gillian Clegg, History Press, 2005
Norwood Pubs, John Coulter, History Press, 2006
Inns, Taverns and Pubs of the London Borough of Sutton: Their History and Architecture, A.J. Crowe, London Borough of Sutton, 1980
The Pubs of Dulwich and Herne Hill, The Dulwich and Herne Hill Society, 2016
London Made Us: A Memoir of a Shape-Shifting City, Robert Elms, Canongate Books, 2020
A Selection of London's Most Interesting Pubs, David Gammell, Woodfield Publishing, 1992
Victorian Pubs, Mark Girouard, Yale University Press, 1984
A Guide to London's Best Pubs, Martin Green, Virgin Books, 1982
Evening Standard Guide to London Pubs, Martin Green and Tony White, Pan Books Ltd, 1973
The London Pub, Peter Haydon and Chris Coe, New Holland Publishers, 2003
Known Treasures and Hidden Gems: Guide to the Pubs of London, Peter Haydon, CAMRA Books, 1996
Pubs, Inns and Taverns of Kingston, Richard F. Holmes, Wildhern Press, 2010
Pubs, Inns and Taverns of Richmond, Richard F. Holmes, Echo Library, 2016
City of London Pubs, Johnny Homer, Amberley Publishing, 2016
Clerkenwell and Islington Pubs, Johnny Homer, Amberley Publishing, 2017
East End Pubs, Johnny Homer, Amberley Publishing, 2018

Southwark Pubs, Johnny Homer, Amberley Publishing, 2017
The Traditional Pubs of London's East End (in 2000), J.P. Hughes, Lost Century Books, 2001
Tales from the Two Puddings: Stratford, London's Olympic City, in the 1960s, Eddie Johnson, Fifty First State Press, 2012
Public House, David Knight and Cristina Monteiro (editors), Open City, 2021
Evening Standard London Pub Guide 1995, Angus McGill, Pavilion Books Ltd, 1994
Evening Standard London Pub Guide 1996, Angus McGill, Pavilion Books Ltd, 1995
Evening Standard London Pub Guide 1997, Angus McGill, Evening Standard Books, 1996
The Rough Pub Guide: A Celebration of the Great British Boozer, Paul Moody and Robin Turner, Orion, 2008
The Romance of Thames-Side Taverns, Glyn H. Morgan, Essex Countryside, 1969
Nairn's London, Ian Nairn, Penguin Classics, 2014
Inn and Around London: History of Young's Pubs, Helen Osborn, 1991
Forever Young's: A historical guide to some of Britain's best pubs, Helen Osborn, 2004
Lost Pubs of Bexley: Pubs created after 1830 and since closed, James Packer, Bexley Council, 2005
Haunted Pub Guide, Guy Lyon Playfair, Cassell Illustrated, 1987
The Taverns in the Town, H.E. Popham, Robert Hale Ltd, 1937
Best Pubs in London, A CAMRA guide, Roger Protz, CAMRA Books, 1989
London Pubs, Alan Reeve-Jones, T. Batsford Ltd, 1964
Taverns in Town, Alan and Michael Roulstone, Balfour/Travellers Rest, 1973
Barnet Pubs: Another Round, Richard Selby, 2008
Alka-Seltzer guide to the Pubs of London, R.M. Smith (ed), Bayard London, 1976
Evening Standard – The London Pub and Bar Guide 1998, Edward Sullivan, Evening Standard Books, 1997
Evening Standard – The London Pub and Bar Guide 1999, Edward Sullivan, Simon and Schuster Ltd, 1998
Derelict London, Paul Talling, Random House Books, 2008
Smell of Broken Glass, Sean Tracey, 1973
London Inns and Taverns, Leopold Wagner, George Allen and Unwin, 1924
More London Inns and Taverns, Leopold Wagner, George Allen and Unwin, 1925
Pubs of North Lambeth: A Guide to the Pubs and Street Corners of Waterloo, Kennington and Vauxhall Today and Yesterday, Peter John Walker, 1989
Pubs of Wimbledon Town (Past and Present), Clive Whichelow, Enigma Publishing, 2021
Pubs of Wimbledon Village (Past and Present), Clive Whichelow, Enigma Publishing, 2008
Fancyapint? In London, John Blake Publishing, 2006
Time Out Guide: Pubs and Bars 1998/1999, Time Out Guides, 1998

Time Out Guide: Pubs and Bars 1999/2000, Time Out Guides, 1999
Time Out Guide: Pubs and Bars 2000/2001, Time Out Guides, 2000
Time Out Guide: Pubs and Bars 2001/2002, Time Out Guides, 2001
Time Out Guide: Pubs and Bars 2002/2003, Time Out Guides, 2002
Time Out Guide: Pubs and Bars 2003/2004, Time Out Guides, 2003
Time Out Guide: Pubs and Bars 2004/2005, Time Out Guides, 2004
Time Out Guide: Bars, Pubs and Clubs 2005/2006, Time Out Guides, 2005
Time Out Guide: Bars, Pubs and Clubs 2006/2007, Time Out Guides, 2006
Time Out Guide: Bars, Pubs and Clubs 2007/2008, Time Out Guides, 2007

INDEX